LEADERSHIP IN SCHOOLS

Leadership in Schools

DENYS JOHN

Special Lecturer
University of Bristol School of Education
formerly
Headmaster, Nailsea School, Avon

HEINEMANN EDUCATIONAL BOOKS
LONDON

Heinemann Educational Books Ltd
22 Bedford Square, London WC1B 3HH

LONDON EDINBURGH MELBOURNE AUCKLAND
HONG KONG SINGAPORE KUALA LUMPUR NEW DELHI
IBADAN NAIROBI JOHANNESBURG
EXETER (NH) KINGSTON PORT OF SPAIN

British Library Cataloguing in Publication Data

John, Denys
    Leadership in schools. — (Organization in schools).
    1. School management and organization — Great
    Britain
    I. Title   II. Series
    371.2'00941   LB2901

    ISBN 0-435-80280-1

Typeset by the Castlefield Press of High Wycombe
in 11/12pt Baskerville, and printed in Great Britain by
Richard Clay (The Chaucer Press) Ltd,
Bungay, Suffolk

Contents

Foreword

The underlying purpose of the whole of the Heinemann Organization in Schools Series is to help schools use the freedom that there is in the devolved British system of education to create and to develop schools in which the organization assists the educational experience. Each book has been written by a different author, and from a different point of view; each book is personal, in that it grows out of the individual author's own experience, observation, and study. Nevertheless, the series is planned so that the volumes are complementary, between them covering the overlapping aspects of school organization.

If the theme of the series is that school organization matters, it is also true that leadership is presented throughout the series as of great importance, not merely the leadership of the head of a separate institution, but also the leadership of the many others who take responsibility. A number of the series titles highlight this, especially *School Decision-Making, Pastoral Care, Head of Department, School Evaluation*, and *Comprehensive Values*. The present volume, however, is devoted entirely to a consideration of the practical implications of the meaning of leadership in a school, and is therefore a key book in the series.

The author, Denys John, is in a special position to be able to write such a study: not only was he a headteacher for twenty-five years, seeing Nailsea School through from a Grammar School to a Comprehensive one, but he collaborated with Elizabeth Richardson in her lengthy and detailed study of the management implications of those changes (published in *The Teacher, The School and the Task of Management*). In this new book he brings together considerable personal experience with wide theoretical study to produce a work which is both eminently practical and at the same time a sensitive personal document.

MICHAEL MARLAND

Author's Acknowledgements

I would like to acknowledge the debt that I owe to all the teaching and non-teaching staff who served at Nailsea School at any time between 1959 and 1976. It was during discussions with them, whether individual or corporate, formal or informal, that many of the ideas examined in this book were developed. Some of these ideas grew from suggestions made by Nailsea colleagues. Others were formulated as a result of the challenges they made to traditional perspectives and practices, challenges which, though often relentless, were invariably patient and constructive.

The stimulus for our most fruitful staff discussions was provided by the consultancy which Elizabeth Richardson offered to my colleagues and me between the years 1968 and 1971 and which was recorded in her book *The Teacher, the School and the Task of Management.* Her own contribution, like that of all the best teachers, was never prescriptive and never perceived as judgemental. She had the skill and experience to perceive the fundamental issues and the courage to ask the unavoidable questions.

During the late 1960s and early 1970s, when reorganization of secondary education was gaining impetus, the comprehensive schools committee of the Headmasters' Association (now the Secondary Heads' Association) undertook a thorough exploration of the new demands being made upon the heads of schools and of ways of trying to meet them. Many of the views expressed in this book were first generated in those committee discussions, and I am grateful for the experience of working with that committee.

Some of the concepts and practices concerned with running a secondary school which are discussed in this book would have seemed totally unsuitable and unworkable to me when I first became a headmaster twenty-eight years ago. Such

new approaches are not always welcomed by all the various
groups which have an interest in a school. Changes which
seem contrary to time-honoured traditions need to be approached with caution. For this reason I must finally express
my gratitude to the governors of Nailsea School, to the LEAs
of both Somerset and Avon, to the parents, and especially
perhaps to the generations of pupils for the tolerant adaptability that they showed, and for the confident encouragement that they offered to the teachers and to me as we tried
to bring our procedures into harmony with changing needs,
even on those occasions when our attempts seemed less
beneficial than we had hoped.

DENYS JOHN

1 Relevance and the Current Scene

Much of the anxiety that pervades modern society has its origin in uncertainties about leadership and authority. There always seems to be either too much, interfering with individual freedom, which is perceived as tyrannical; or not enough, so that anarchy and licence seem to leave us less protected than we think we have a right to be. In fact it is not a case of either/or, but of both grievances seeming valid simultaneously. 'They' have never been more criticized and distrusted, whether 'they' are the Government, the Commissioners of Inland Revenue, the Health Service Administration, the heads of schools, the managers of industry or the leaders of trades unions. The need for their very existence is questioned, and the word 'leadership' is avoided as embarrassing. It remains true that there is a strong recognition that our complex society requires leaders, and anger is occasioned more often because we consider they are not doing enough than because we think they are doing too much. Perhaps the biggest misunderstandings are about the nature and purpose of authority and about our perceptions of how and why 'authorities' act in the way they do.

It is ironical that in an age when technology has provided so many new and relatively easy instruments of communication, disillusionment, bred from a feeling of isolated helplessness, is so common. The disillusionment leads to the assumption that leadership means power and privilege, and that people in authority are there because they think they know best and because they want advantages for themselves which others may not share. The isolation means that leaders are perceived as ignorant of the needs of ordinary mortals and insensitive to their problems. It also means that the actions of leaders appear arbitrary and dictatorial. It is significant that the only leader who received widespread recognition (at least during the war years) was Winston

Churchill. His task (to defeat Hitler) was clear cut, simple in conception, and universally supported by the citizens of his country. His policies and actions could easily be related to his task of enabling the country to fulfil its aims, and could be judged by that criterion. If Churchill was a 'great leader', it was at least partly because his task was so clear that communication between him and the rest of the country was not a problem. The nostalgia which many older people feel for the war years owes much of its attraction to the sense of common purpose shared by all members and epitomized by the leadership. In such circumstances people saw no cause to question the value of leadership, or to interpret its activities as arbitrary or its motives as self-interested.

It would appear, then, that leadership is most likely to be effective when it is perceived as pursuing aims approved by the members and using methods that appear to the members to be appropriate.

In any organization there may well be present two conditions which render effective leadership difficult to achieve. The first condition is the absence of easy, direct channels of communication in both directions between the leadership and the members. The second is the disparate and conflicting aims of individuals and groups within the organization.

'Easy and direct channels of communication' is often interpreted as simply meaning a better internal telephone system, a tannoy apparatus or frequent informal meetings between the leader and members in the corridors, canteens and common rooms. While all of these are required, they are not sufficient. Time, space and organization must also be mobilized to bring people together, to explore their aspirations and the paths which might lead to their achievement. Elizabeth Richardson describes this work in these words:

> The key to the problem of communication between pupils and teachers may therefore be found in the kind of work the staff are prepared to do within their own working groups, through open exploration of their own internal conflicts and through their own struggle to discover which are the real and important divergencies between them and which are spurious. Yet the increasing size of the schools makes this task more and more difficult, even while it is becoming more and more necessary if the problems which are arising between staff and pupils are to be understood.[1]

[1] Richardson, E., *The Teacher, the School and the Task of Management*, Heinemann, 1973, p. 11.

Elizabeth Richardson here points to the need for effective consultative machinery through which teachers of all levels of responsibility and experience may explore the real and the assumed, the important and the irrelevant in the differences between them, whether these concern assumptions, aims or methods. Without such effective consultation, leadership is bound to be helpless, as a substantial proportion of the staff group will deny the leadership any right or justification to act on its behalf.

When basic aims and assumptions remain disparate even after protracted discussion, the leader of a department or a school is in a difficult situation. Comprehensive schools which have been able to develop gradually from a single institution suffer less from this problem than those which are the result of mergers between a number of schools, some of which may have been unwilling partners in the new enterprise. Often an improvement comes accidentally by the sinking of differences in the face of a common threat from outside. A hostile local press or parish council may do for a school what Hitler achieved in 1940 for the population of Britain, and what GCE examiners may have achieved for a fifth-form teacher who could not gain the co-operation of his class in earlier years. Aware of the importance of common aims and assumptions, leaders sometimes seek to *impose* their own upon the members, or alternatively to mobilize an external enemy. Members themselves have been known to conjure up fantasy enemies and invent conspiracy theories in order to create the unity that they, too, desire. In this way they hope to avoid the need for a unity imposed by the coercive power of the leadership. The use of coercion and of fantasy enemies is equally ineffective in the long term. Coercion produces the appearance of outward conformity without mobilizing the inner resources of the membership. The identification of external enemies, whether real or imagined, channels group energies into the task of refuting, discrediting or defeating the enemy but away from the primary task of the institution. It follows that leaders and managers have no long-term effective alternative to creating conditions in which the members themselves can formulate and realize group aspirations.

If our late twentieth-century society possessed a more coherent view of leadership and of the nature of authority, there would be a chance for more constructive relationships to develop in our institutions. Too often organizations are disrupted or gravely handicapped by the different and contradictory assumptions held about the purpose of leadership and the authority of the individual.

The legacy of the past makes it difficult for us today to create and hold on to a constructive view of leadership. The practice of slavery, the tyranny of the industrial revolution, the continuing association of power with inherited wealth or privilege and the experience of Nazi and Fascist regimes induce our present society to regard leadership as exploitative rather than facilitative. No doubt the behaviour of some, even many, leaders helps to confirm this interpretation. Even if it did not, and even if leaders always behaved as facilitators, attitudes towards them would retain an element of resentment, which is increasingly seen as natural, along with a desire to co-operate, which is seen as unnatural. The present danger is that the resentment is frequently felt to be fully justified to the exclusion of co-operation. Many people feel that leaders are there to be frustrated as much as possible, and totally destroyed when the opportunity presents itself. The assumption is that we have a choice only between tyranny and anarchy and that, on the whole, anarchy is preferable.

The opposition to the very idea of leadership is connected with our perception of the authority of the individual. If the word 'authority' is held to be synonymous with 'power' or 'privilege', then it becomes an attribute of leaders which is denied to the rank and file. In practice no co-operative enterprise (and the effectiveness of our society depends to a great extent upon the existence of these) can achieve the task entrusted to it without each member possessing, recognizing and exercising his own authority and having it recognized by others. The sense of the word 'authority' in this context refers to the respect accorded to a member's skills and knowledge when these are directed effectively to the performance of his share of a corporate task in such a way that the tasks of others are more easily and effectively fulfilled. A recognition of our own authority enables us to respect the authority of others. Elizabeth Richardson expressed the other face of the same coin in an article in *The Times Educational Supplement* of 19 October 1973 under the title (given by the paper's editorial staff) 'Knowing who is boss': 'It is only by coming to terms with the authority that is outside ourselves that we can discover the authority that is inside.'

The absence of a coherent view about leadership and authority not only handicaps institutional relations but also confuses and frustrates the individual member by undermining his sense of 'oneness' or 'integrity'. This is particularly true of institutions in the caring services such as schools. The whole ethos of society seems to accord value and merit to ambition and to readiness to undertake leadership. The young teacher 'at the bottom of the ladder' already has to contend with his own ambivalent feelings about his right to assume leadership in relation to his pupils. The children themselves share these ambivalent feelings towards the authority of the teacher. On the whole, at least in primary schools and in the upper streams and sets of the secondary schools, the facilitating purpose of a teacher's leadership is sufficiently conspicuous for the relationship to be accepted. It may not even be considered to be leadership or management at all (though an important aim of this book will be to try to demonstrate that such it is).

It is when a role entails leadership of other teachers that confusion about it may deter some of the most dedicated and sensitive teachers from seeking promotion — not simply because they see it as necessarily entailing the use of coercive powers over others in exchange for privileges which they are embarrassed to accept. They also believe that leadership enforces the abandonment of all humane feelings and personal relationships in exchange for mechanical, repetitive, administrative tasks. Of course the pressures to accept promotion are exceedingly strong. Financial rewards as well as the satisfactions arising from the exercise of skills which have been acquired ensure that vacancies are filled. It remains true that, having accepted a leadership role in relation to other teachers, a head of department, a pastoral head, a deputy or a head of a school may remain uncertain of how to fulfil his new responsibilities without sacrificing those principles which first induced him to become a teacher. Different strategies may be adopted by teachers in such a situation in an effort to escape from the dilemma. Some may deny the very existence of their leadership role and choose to regard promotion as merely reward in financial and status terms for past competence. Others accept the initiating, persuading parts of leadership but evade the tougher aspects of decision-making and staff-appraisal since the latter are, in their perception, inevitably autocratic. When this strategy is adopted, a middle or top manager may sometimes adopt an excessive form of informality in order to dissolve the assumed barrier between himself and colleagues. This may sometimes extend to the abandonment of all privileges — not solely of status-based irrelevant ones (a fully justified course of action) but also of those supplied for the more effective conduct of his role. Open access may thus be granted to telephones, private offices and other equipment, sometimes to the detriment of the effective leadership of a department. Yet others make strenuous efforts to divide themselves as 'persons' from their role as leaders. In their first capacity as persons, they may designate places and activities in which they are Bill or Harry, Jane or Joan — in the Staff Common Room or the local pub — in which it is prohibited to talk shop and they can be pals with their colleagues. In their official role, they then feel able — in the department or behind their desks — to behave with a graver formality, sometimes acting with a ruthlessness not necessarily implicit in their role and an arbitrariness which they consider inseparable from leadership.

One of the most frequent complaints made by teachers is the apparent absence of sufficient opportunities for training in preparation for leadership roles. This complaint ignores the fundamental truth that leadership itself is a continuum of opportunity. With promotion, the boundaries of responsibilities widen but the principles remain the same. The role of the classroom teacher is the embryo of the role of the head of department. This in its turn is the foundation for a proper understanding of the roles of the deputy head or the head. This is certainly not to say that there is no place for courses in management. It does mean, however, that a new understanding of the nature of leadership makes the school itself (with the relationships it represents and the opportunities for participation which it presents), into a proper location for and instrument of training for promotion. This will be most successful when members of an organization at all levels of responsibility conceive of their functions as focusing on the development of the personal and corporate effectiveness of the groups for which they are responsible. If they define their leadership in these terms and conduct it at all times with openness and an acknowledgement of the reality of feelings as well as reasoning, 'staff development' can become intrinsic in the routine work of the school.

Consultation about what shall be changed and what shall be preserved unchanged is thus inseparable from the continuous process of re-education within the staff group . . . Every staff group has within it the ingredients of a kind of continuous educational workshop.[1]

[1] Richardson, E., *The Teacher, the School and the Task of Management*, Heinemann, 1973, p. 314.

2 Organizations and the Nature of Leadership

In the last chapter the claim was made that organizations mostly depend upon co-operative activity in which leadership has an important part to play. The effectiveness of the organization and of all its members is likely to be enhanced when there is a clear understanding of and agreement about the purpose of the organization and about the mode or style of leadership in the different parts of the organization. It is this mode or style that constitutes the 'climate' of an institution.

This chapter will examine a possible theoretical model intended to provide teachers in secondary schools with a coherent overview of the main elements involved. Theoretical models do not, of course, in themselves necessarily command understanding or respect for their appropriateness, nor do they alone make institutions and those who work in them more effective. It may nevertheless be useful to study some theoretical systems derived from the study of actual enterprises. These suggest that a shared understanding of and a commitment to the goals of an organization are related to its effectiveness and are associated more with certain modes of leadership than with others. Moreover, different organizational climates are more suited to the achievement of some purposes than others.

A conceptual framework which has proved helpful is the one described by A. K. Rice in *The Enterprise and its Environment* (1963)[1] which is further elaborated in *Systems of Organisation*.[2] Usually referred to as 'Open-System Theory', this approach identifies a number of characteristics held in

[1] Rice, A. K., *The Enterprise and its Environment*, Tavistock Publications, 1963.
[2] Miller, E. J. and Rice, A. K., *Systems of Organisation*, Tavistock Publications, 1967.

common by individual organisms, groups and institutions. Rice described organisms and institutions as constituting an inner world existing in an outer environment. The distinction between the inner and the outer world — i.e. between the 'enterprise' and its environment — is marked by the existence of a boundary. If the enterprise is to survive it must exchange materials with its environment. All institutions take in 'raw materials' of various kinds. Inside the boundary, various processes are set up which exert changes upon the materials imported. The changed product is then exported into the environment. Rice referred to this as the 'import– conversion– export' process. He saw this process as applicable not only to the total organization but also and equally to sub-systems within the total institution.

Each institution has, then, its own import–conversion– export process, and this constitutes its 'primary task — the task that it must perform to survive'. For schools, the primary task is to accept pupils, to provide means by which those pupils can develop into educated people, and to pass them on to society or to other institutions. For Rice, 'primary' is intended to be an exclusive term, and there can be only one primary task at any given time. He concedes however that, particularly in times of rapid change, there may be more than one task, and which task is perceived as dominant may change at different times or be perceived differently by the environment of the enterprise from the way the enterprise itself views it. Thus the community surrounding a school may see its primary task to be the production of examination successes, while the teachers may see it as the development of co-operative members of a community — or vice versa at varying times.

The importance of this concept of primary task lies in the insights it provides about the functions of leadership and the decisions required about the necessary resources and the sub-systems to be set up to accomplish the task. Rice and Miller refer to the fact that 'the members of an enterprise depend on their managers to identify their tasks and to provide the resources for task performance'.

The leadership function is seen as placed on the boundary of any institution or any sub-system within the institution. The leader is equally concerned with the external environment, within which is situated the group for which he is responsible and the internal life of that group. Consequently the leader faces in two directions simultaneously. In defining for his group the nature of their primary task, he must heed the sources of the 'raw material' imported by his enterprise and the destination of the finished products. Changes in sources of material or the nature of the 'market' can have profound consequences for the way in which the enterprise constitutes its operating systems.

It has been pointed out that the primary task of a secondary school is to receive pupils from families and from primary schools, to turn them into 'educated' young people by the use of teachers, ideas, materials and equipment (which are also imported), and to export these educated young people to a market consisting of employers, colleges and universities. There have been radical changes in recent years in all the elements which constitute this process. Firstly, the pupils imported by a comprehensive school represent a different range of achievement from those previously imported by grammar or secondary-modern schools separately. Moreover, changes in primary-school methods have also altered the emphasis in the experience of those pupils before the transfer. Secondly, the nature of the primary task of producing educated young people is itself uncertain and subject to widely differing interpretations. It became apparent during the 'Great Debate' of 1976–77 that there is no consensus of opinion about what an 'educated young person' is. The features of an educated person identified by different people vary widely, even when those people represent similar consumer interests. The opinions of these representatives of the environment which receives the products of the schools are not to be dismissed simply because they are not unanimous. It is the responsibility of leadership in schools (governing bodies and LEAs in consultation with heads) to note the kinds of demands being made by the community upon schools and to negotiate broad agreement about them.

To do this there must be co-operation between the maintaining authority, the governors, the teachers, the parents and pupils, and other representatives of the community served by the school. This clarification is not a simple task. Many of the aims advocated by different interests are incompatible with each other, and this is probably inevitable in as complex a task as that of educating young people. In the absence of an analysis of what 'educating young people' means for any particular school, the perception of teachers and pupils of the nature of their roles and also the whole internal organization of the school may be out of date. They are likely to reflect practices and traditions which are no longer appropriate to the changed environment and the different intake of pupils.

In writing of leadership as involving the task of relating an enterprise to its environment, references to the enterprise as 'the school' and identification of the environment with a surrounding community may obscure the conclusion that the same features are characteristic of the leadership of the sub-systems within the boundary of the school. The subject departments, the year groups or houses, the individual classes and tutor groups are all first- or second-order sub-systems with their own stated or assumed primary tasks and their own leadership roles. For them, too, the task or tasks require definition, and in defining these tasks, the environment of the classes or departments or pastoral groupings is important. Relating the work of a department to that of other departments, of a class to that of other classes, is the responsibility of leadership. The way which this 'relating' or co-ordinating is perceived will then influence the way in which the leadership of the sub-system concerned organizes the methods, activities and resources within the sub-system. This, then, is the dual task of leadership at every level, whether top management (governors, head and deputies), middle management (heads of faculties, departments, year groups or houses) or junior management (subject teachers and form tutors).

The use of the term 'level' as applied to management or leadership may be questioned by some both inside and outside the teaching profession. Indeed much of the philosophy implicit in comprehensive education appears incompatible with the principle of any kind of hierarchy. Equality of opportunity and equality of value, which are understandable and perhaps intrinsic elements of comprehensive philosophy, appear to conflict with the acceptance of hierarchical levels.

A further objection to hierarchical systems is that the greater the control they exert over communication and over the distribution of tasks, rights and obligations, the less they are susceptible to change. Griffiths points out that 'Open Systems display a progressive segregation. This process occurs when the system divides into a hierarchical order of subordinate systems, which gain a certain independence of each other.'[1] Another (and perhaps a consequent) characteristic of open systems is that they 'maintain themselves in steady states (a constant ratio is maintained among the components of the system) whereas change calls for the establishment of new ratios among the components of the system.' Although change may occur in such systems, it is infrequent and is usually the result of pressures from outside, from a supra-system or from the environment. 'Since organizations are open systems, they have a self-regulating characteristic which causes them to revert to the original state following a minor change made to meet the demands of the supra-system.' Elsewhere Griffiths states the proposition: 'The more hierarchical the structure of an organization, the less the possibility of change.' Similarly Professor Hoyle detects changes in the authority pattern of schools and sees a movement towards collegial authority as favourable to innovation.[2]

Now schools must maintain the fundamentals of their steady state if they are to continue to accomplish the specific purpose for which society established them. For this they require a hierarchical structure. However, simultaneously, the changing nature of the demands made upon them by the knowledge explosion, by research into how children learn, and by the technological and social revolution, obliges schools to be flexible enough to be able to change. Burns and Stalker suggest a theoretical outline which describes how the same management system may be used to meet either stable conditions or changing conditions, or a mixture of both kinds of conditions. These two manners of using a management system constitute sets of patterns which 'represent a polarity, not a dichotomy . . . The relation of one form to the other is elastic so that a concern oscillating between relative stability and relative change may also oscillate between the two forms.'[3]

The two forms identified by Burns and Stalker are called 'mechanistic' and 'organic' forms. The mechanistic form

[1] Griffiths, D. E., 'Administrative Theory and Change in Organizations' in Miles, M. B. (ed.), *Innovation in Education*, Teachers' College, Columbia University, 1964, p. 430.

[2] Hoyle, E., *Problems of Curriculum Innovation II*, Unit 17, Course E283, Open University, 1972, p. 23.

[3] Burns, T. and Stalker, G. M., *The Management of Innovation*, Tavistock Publications, 1961, p. 119.

is appropriate to stable conditions and emphasizes specialized differentiation of tasks designated by immediate superiors, a hierarchical structure of control, authority and communication, insistence on loyalty and obedience, and separation of individual tasks from the ends of the concern as a whole. The organic form, which is appropriate to changing conditions, fresh problems and unforeseen requirements, is marked by the contribution of knowledge and experience to the common task, the diffusion of responsibility, a network of control, authority and communication (the latter sideways rather than upwards and downwards), no imputation of omniscience to the head of the organization, and emphasis upon information and advice rather than instructions and decisions.

There are two points of some importance in this analysis which might easily be misinterpreted. The first is that Burns and Stalker do not invite organizations to adopt either form of polarity in its pure state, as virtually all must maintain a degree of stability in some respects while changing in other respects. The second is that the association of the word 'hierarchy' with mechanistic forms of management is not an argument in favour of abandoning diversified levels of responsibility. Burns and Stalker made this clear by adding:

> One important corollary to be attached to this account is that, while organic systems are not hierarchic in the same sense as are mechanistic, they remain stratified. Positions are differentiated according to seniority — i.e. greater expertise. The lead in joint decisions is frequently taken by seniors, but it is an essential presumption of the organic system that the lead, i.e. 'authority' is taken by whoever shows himself most informed and capable, i.e. the 'best authority'. The location of authority is settled by consensus.

While leadership and responsibility, therefore, in the organic system are more widely shared, and meet the requirements of change, they do not replace the formal structure of responsibility for the tasks of maintaining the organization, nor, of course, are members of the formal structure excluded from playing a part in innovation. This is a point of great importance in ensuring job satisfaction, since system innovation tends to be more stimulating and rewarding than system maintenance. (This is referred to in Chapter 5, entitled 'Roles', under the headings of 'Coherence', 'Creativity' and 'Credibility', and also in the opening section, which refers to the concept of administration.)

A move towards a more organic mode of management is also sometimes seen as a device to by-pass the formal system (identified with anti-change forces) by the institution of 'temporary systems' (such as committees, conferences, in-service training centres, workshops, visiting teams, consultancies). Miles clearly advocates this. 'For many reasons, permanent systems — whether persons, groups or organisations — find it difficult to change themselves.'[1] He sees this as stemming from their expenditure of energy on routine goal-directed operations, which leaves little or no energy for 'diagnosis, planning, innovation, deliberate change and growth'. The deliberate establishment of temporary systems in our schools is illustrated by the increasing use of study groups, working parties and staff conferences. They must not, however, be relied upon for the purpose of 'by-passing' the formal system in the sense of preparing proposals of which the formal system is left in ignorance, or for the purpose of depriving people in designated positions of responsibility of any innovative role, relegating them to entirely implementational or routine tasks. 'By-passing' of the formal structure is sometimes resorted to in desperation when the latter seems incapable of changing its procedures. It is described by Burns and Stalker as follows:

> So in some concerns, there developed an ambiguous system of an official hierarchy of power and responsibility, and a clandestine or open system of pair relationships between the head of the concern and some dozen of persons at different positions below him in the management. The head of the concern would be overloaded with work, and senior managers, whose standing depended on the operation of the formal system, would feel aggrieved at being by-passed.[2]

Elizabeth Richardson[3] saw an objection to the use of temporary systems in their tendency to divert attention from serious examination of relationships in the formal structure:

> Setting up voluntary working parties, while it appears to be authorizing people to take . . . initiatives (to use themselves more fully, finding greater satisfactions and developing new skills) can in fact seriously obstruct the work that needs to be done between colleagues

---

[1] Miles, M. B., 'On Temporary Systems' in Miles, M. B. (ed.), *Innovation in Education*, Teachers' College, Columbia University, 1964, p. 443.

[2] op. cit., p. ix.

[3] Richardson, E., 'Knowing who is boss', *The Times Educational Supplement*, 19.10.73.

with related and interdependent tasks by blurring the boundaries within which these people are having to work with pupils.

We have examined three problems about temporary systems — firstly, by-passing, secondly, the denial to the formal system of a share in innovation, and thirdly, the diversion of attention from the formal system in which the reality of daily work with pupils takes place. A fourth problem is that temporary systems, by their selective and impermanent nature, are very prone to the charge that they increase the fragmentation of the institution. It is ironic that it is an identical objection to the formal system which often contributes to the desire to move from the formal system into temporary and informal ones. (See Griffiths, op. cit., on 'a hierarchical order of subordinate systems, which gain a certain independence of each other' mentioned earlier in this chapter.) Temporary systems tend to promote policies in which both continuity and coherence are at risk.

On balance I regard the disadvantages of temporary systems as too high a price to pay for their alleged advantages. An attempt to use the formal system in such a way that inertia and 'progressive segregation' are avoided is described in Chapter 7 (Participation and Consultation).

What seems to be needed in schools is a range of leadership responsibilities which are not too rigidly specified and which are interdependent and flexible rather than segregated and bureaucratic. Interaction with colleagues engaged in the same tasks and committed to the same objectives needs to be fostered by formal methods in permanent groups and supplemented by less formal methods in smaller groups. In such a climate 'authority' is not the reserve of certain hierarchical echelons, but is accorded to whoever has the most appropriate expertise. A proper understanding of leadership and authority, of the opportunities and limitations of hierarchies, involves, then, a recognition of one's own responsibility to take the lead in appropriate circumstances (when one possesses the greater information and capability) as well as the need to allow it to pass to others when they possess greater information and capability in a given situation. This is very different from the denial of leadership in oneself or in others, which is merely an evasion of responsibility. A desire for pleasant personal relationships with junior colleagues and for acceptance by them on equal terms must not be allowed to deprive the members of an organization or a sub-system of the leadership which they require for the fulfilment of their responsibilities. Class teachers may be subject to the temptation to deny their leadership in order to be accepted by pupils as 'one of us' rather than as 'one of them'. The irony is that such a denial of role differentiation would deprive the pupils of the leadership they require if they are to gain the fulfilment that comes from being learners.

Conclusion

The 'Open-System' and the 'Organic and Mechanistic' models lead, then, to the identification of a number of features of institutions which need the attention of their members. These features are ones which leaders throughout the organization must be aware of, and bring forward for discussion by the membership group, so that decisions are reached concerning them.

These features are:

1. the nature of the primary task (Task Definition, Chapter 3, and Aims, Chapter 4);
2. the practical policies which require to be implemented in order to fulfil the primary task (Objectives, Chapter 4);
3. a clarification of the roles to be fulfilled by members of the institution in order to discharge the aims and objectives (Roles, Chapter 5);
4. the sub-systems which seem appropriate to enable the institution to fulfil its task (Pastoral and Curricular Sub-Systems, Chapter 6);
5. the establishing of flexible and continuing systems of communication and consultation between all members of the institution and between them and representatives of the environment (Participation and Consultation, Decision-Making, Chapters 7 and 8);
6. the initiation of procedures by which all these are evaluated and kept under review (Evaluation, Chapter 9).

3 Problems of Task Definition in the Comprehensive School

In the last chapter, the 'Open-System Theory' was described briefly as a way of considering the nature of institutions. The main characteristics of institutions were said to be the 'boundary' which separates the organization from its surroundings and the 'import–conversion–export' process which constitutes the 'primary task' of the organization. The primary task for schools is to receive pupils from their families and from other schools, to provide for them experiences designed to promote their growth and understanding, and to 'export' them as educated young adults to employment or further education. There is unlikely to be disagreement that such is the aim. The 1944 Education Act makes it:

> the duty of every local education authority to secure that there should be sufficient schools for providing primary education and secondary education – in schools sufficient in number, character, and equipment to afford all pupils opportunities for education offering such variety of instruction and training as may be desirable in view of their different ages, abilities and aptitudes and of the different periods for which they may be expected to remain at school.

Model Articles of Government declare that the Local Education Authority shall determine the character of the school and its place in the educational system, and that the headteacher shall be responsible to the governors for the general direction of the conduct and curriculum of the school. There is no doubt that schools are intended to educate. However, a definition of education and an analysis of the values which may be involved is much more controversial.

In an article ('Boring and Burnham') in the issue of *The Times Educational Supplement* of 2 June 1978, Gerry Fowler quoted the American political philosopher David Easton, who once defined policy-making as 'the authoritative allocation of values for a society'. Gerry Fowler comments: 'if we look at educational policy-making in Britain . . . we may ask not only whose values, but whose authority?' In the United Kingdom we have a strong tradition of decentralization. We are liable to distrust the Napoleonic approach to policy-making. Indeed the 1944 Education Act emphasized 'such variety of instruction and training as may be desirable'. It seems to have been assumed that the Local Education Authority, the school governors and the headteacher would find no difficulty in reaching agreement about what is to be deemed 'desirable'. In practice LEAs, governors and head-teachers have each accommodated their own views to those of the other parties concerned and policies have 'emerged'. At the present time, this situation reveals at least two major weaknesses. The first weakness is that the policies of an individual school are rarely codified, written down or communicated to all those who have a stake in its activities. Secondly, several parties other than the three mentioned have an important interest in these policies, and yet their participation is not legally protected and may often not occur. These other parties are the parents (whose access to governors may often be tenuous and unorganized), the teachers (who may be fully consulted and have their views represented by the headteacher, but equally who may not), the pupils themselves, and the employers and other interests in the local community served by a school. The importance of the Taylor Report[1] is that it acknowledges the part which can be played by representatives of parents, pupils, teachers and members of the local community in defining for their school the values and assumptions underlying the general way in which it is to be conducted and the knowledge, skills and attitudes of the educated citizen which it is charged to produce. The values and assumptions referred to are a necessary preliminary to defining its task. This is the subject of the present chapter. The knowledge, skills and attitudes constitute the school's goals or aims and will be considered in the next chapter.

Although schools differ in their views about the constituent elements of the curriculum, they may be even more divergent in the values which underlie the policies which they adopt. There are three key areas in which opposing values are in conflict with one another. They are:

[1] DES, *A New Partnership for Our Schools*, HMSO, 1977.

1. national needs and the purpose of schools;
2. the origins of human potential;
3. the nature of motivation.

1. *National needs and the purpose of schools*

On this subject it is possible and logical to take either one of two extreme standpoints. Some would say that a state education service should give priority to the achievement of an acceptable threshold of competence for the majority of children. This might be termed the 'popular' or 'egalitarian' end of the spectrum of beliefs. The opposite extreme viewpoint is to consider the primary purpose of education to be the production of leaders who will fulfil the nation's needs in industry, politics, culture and the professions. This view sets the high success of the few above raising the general level of competence of the many. Adherents of this view emphasize the right of gifted children to reach their potential as well as the benefits which accrue indirectly to the masses from the achievements of outstanding leadership. Opponents of this philosophy call it 'elitist'. Both values may well be held simultaneously by the same people. Indeed most schools would assert that they aim to ensure an acceptable level of general education for all their pupils and also to enable the high fliers to win outstanding success. It is nevertheless possible for the curriculum, the pupil groupings and the distribution of resources to reflect one standpoint much more emphatically than the other. Although a thoroughgoing attempt to achieve one aim tends to undermine and defeat the other, comprehensive schools nevertheless must include both purposes in their general aims and try to reach a balance. The issues must be the subject of discussion among all the interested parties so that the practical policies which any given school adopts can command understanding and acceptance.

2. *The origins of human potential*

This is the old 'nature/nurture' controversy — the endless, unresolved debate about whether 'ability' — or 'intelligence' — (both much-abused words) is genetically or environmentally determined. Most educationists would now accept the opinion of researchers that both heredity and environment play their parts in varying and largely unascertainable proportions. This does not prevent either educationists or the public from holding and expressing opinions on practical issues which derive their bias from assumptions about ability which are primarily deterministic or predominantly developmental. Although few people today would claim that performance is entirely conditioned by inherited characteristics, many, perhaps most of us, would see heredity and early nurture as setting the child in a mould which it is extremely difficult, if not impossible, to change later on. It is this deterministic view which enables us, indeed obliges us, to consider very sympathetically the claims that schools must enable 'gifted' children to reach their 'potential'. The developmental assumption about human potential leans towards the opposite end of the spectrum. It assumes that inherited characteristics are more evenly shared than is sometimes thought and that the influence of relatively poor early learning experiences is not necessarily permanent, but may be compensated for by subsequent enrichment. This developmental standpoint leads to the emphasis upon remedial education and to all the school policies which seek to keep doors open for late developers.

In the absence of any definitive evidence on this question schools tend to vary widely in the position they take up on the 'deterministic/developmental' continuum. Once again it is necessary to identify a point of balance between the extremes of the standpoints which exist. This can best be arrived at by detailed discussion within a staff group and between it and the other parties with a vested interest in a particular school. Without a conscious consideration of this issue resources, teachers, status and esteem may be unfairly distributed, to the detriment of either the poorest or the average or the best performers among the pupils.

3. *The nature of motivation*

There is as great a degree of uncertainty among teachers about competition and co-operation as there is about nature and nurture, and about the relative needs of the nation for leadership and for an educated proletariat. It is a subject in which value-judgements and moral attitudes deriving from religious and philosophical beliefs play a part. On the one hand there is a common belief, not confined to the middle class, that human beings produce their best efforts under the spur of competition. Success is seen as the result of the meritorious use of will-power. It is better deserved if achieved by surmounting obstacles and by surpassing competitors. Competition is considered to promote the highly desirable qualities of independence and self-reliance. On the other hand many would argue that co-operation and solidarity with others are qualities which most people need in their daily work more than independence and self-reliance. They would say that will-power and determination are the result of achievement more than the cause of it. Competition only works where the participants start with truly equal chances. Opponents of a competitive ideology would claim that children in schools rarely start with equal chances and that it is unrealistic, unfair and unfeeling to expect them to exert will-power in a race which many of them feel they are doomed to lose.

Most schools adopt policies some of which are based upon the competitive assumption and some on the co-operative assumption. The general public is divided on the question (though it is impossible to say in what proportions). Consequently they are confused about where the schools really stand. If schools are to gain and retain the confidence of their local communities this question needs to be discussed so that there is a common understanding about the balance which is considered appropriate between the two extreme dangers in which competition becomes a rat race and co-operation a feather bed.

On the three subjects of the purpose of schools, the origin of potential and the nature of motivation, certain viewpoints tend to coalesce as they provide mutual reinforcement for each other. The elitist purpose finds support in a deterministic assumption and a competitive morality. Similarly the egalitarian purpose is buttressed by a developmental assumption and a co-operative morality. It is probably true that the national consensus up to the 1950s was largely elitist/deterministic/competitive and found its expression in the selective bipartite system of grammar and secondary-modern schools. Opposition to re-organization of secondary education on comprehensive lines derived much of its impetus from this disjunction of philosophies. Whether it created the comprehensive movement or was created by it, the egalitarian/developmental/co-operative philosophy has certainly gained ground in the last two decades. Nevertheless it has co-existed with the former beliefs rather than replacing them in the minds of individual teachers, administrators and parents, as well as in society generally.

Comprehensive education became national policy under the Labour government and was expressed in 1965 in Circular 10 of that year. The wording of that circular seems to show that comprehensive education was considered exclusively in terms of the abolition of selection at the age of 11 for different types of schools, and that the preoccupation was with buildings and forms of organization to match available accommodation. There was no examination in that circular or elsewhere of the educational beliefs implicit in the replacement of the bipartite system by comprehensive schools. It seems in retrospect that it was assumed that the traditional beliefs would be equally appropriate in the new setting, or that comprehensive re-organization was purely an administrative change which had nothing to do with educational theory.

Faced with the need to make a vast number of decisions about the internal organization and curricula of the new schools, teachers were left without explicit guidance. There was, as in a detective story, only one clue afforded them. This they could mark, digest and pursue to its logical conclusion, or ignore as a red herring. The clue was the abolition of selection at 11+. It constituted a postponement of the educational device (i.e. separate schools) by which some children were to be segregated from others and treated differently. It therefore seemed to many comprehensive schoolteachers to be an invitation to reduce and postpone other differentiating devices which were traditional in the former separate secondary schools of the bipartite system. If no such invitation was really intended, these teachers, uprooted from their former institutions and faced with pupil and parent expectations that they were unfamiliar with, asked themselves why such a massive upheaval was necessary to effect such minimal change.

Of course, many teachers did feel that re-organization was merely a cynical political manoeuvre to assuage the wrath of parents whose children had failed the 11+. Their educational, social, cultural and philosophical beliefs remained the same as before. The schools in which they taught also remained, under one roof or even more markedly if on split sites, the same as before the re-organization.

Other teachers examined more closely the postponement of differentiation between children and, gradually and to varying extents, they re-appraised their basic educational and philosophical beliefs. On the whole, grammar-school teachers, who had enjoyed greater esteem as the educators of a future elite, may have been more identified than secondary-modern schoolteachers with an elitist/deterministic/competitive package of assumptions, and may have had to face a greater revolution in their ideas. When they did face it, and if they accepted the presumed reasons for delaying segregation of certain children at 11, then they tended to adopt more and more of the assumptions which have been described as 'egalitarian/developmental/co-operative'.

Meanwhile educational researchers were pursuing studies of child development, were re-examining the concept of intelligence, documenting behaviour patterns of pupils in various school groupings and social cultures and recording children's responses to the schools' systems of incentives and deterrents. Probably none of the studies totally disposed of elitist/deterministic/competitive assumptions, but they weakened teachers' confidence in their complete and exclusive validity, while presenting for consideration assumptions of a more egalitarian/developmental/co-operative kind.

At the present time teachers seem to hesitate between both forms of belief. The mixed economy which the majority of our comprehensive schools represent satisfies neither side in the political battle which has been waged about comprehensive education. Governments, both national and local, and of both the two main political parties, seem now to accept the broad principle of comprehensive education and the abolition of the 11+, thereby appearing to endorse the egalitarian/developmental/co-operative assumptions; and, on the other hand, governments also seek to maintain a public examination system which (whether the present dual system of GCE and CSE or the proposed GCSE with papers set at different levels of ability) has the principal aim of classifying educational performance. This has a strong back-wash tendency to encourage segregated groupings and differentiated curricular patterns. It may be argued that such an examination system is not incompatible with an egalitarian/developmental/co-operative philosophy, since pupils only sit public examinations when their school course is virtually at an end. However, the effect of this differentiating examination system is not limited to pupils' last months at school. Preparation for it often extends back at least two and sometimes three years, and imposes a need for differentiation between pupils at the age of 13 or 14 which is more elitist/deterministic/competitive than egalitarian/developmental and co-operative. Where possible many comprehensive teachers try to postpone selection for different examinations until the last moment (January of the fifth year) by the use of Mode 3 syllabuses.

The existence of the independent, fee-paying schools also influences comprehensive school policies. The selectivity and the goals of independent schools are in the main inspired by the elitist/deterministic/competitive package of beliefs. The esteem in which they are held by large sectors of society and the comparisons which are made between their achievements and those of comprehensive schools ensure that the latter retain many elements of the same philosophy. Thus the comprehensive schools are urged by the logic of their very nature to move towards the egalitarian/developmental and co-operative philosophy and by the examination system and the existence of the independent sector to move in the opposite direction. Every school seeks its own compromise. They are therefore all different, and this in itself is a source of complaint.[1]

We now come to consider in what ways these philosophies have practical consequences on schools.

Differentiating devices

It has been suggested that the essence of comprehensive education is the reduction and postponement of variations in the treatment of children or of provision for them which reflect (and intentionally or unintentionally reinforce) observed or assumed differences in their performance.

The variations in treatment and provision are generally inspired by assumptions that performance is largely predetermined by heredity and infant nurture, that pupils, however initially disadvantaged, will struggle competitively

[1] See DES, *Education in Schools: a consultative document* Cmnd 6869, HMSO, 1977: the section headed 'Areas of Concern'.

to excel if they possess the requisite qualities of character (also inherited?), and that the primary purpose of schools is to identify and foster the talents of the comparative few who are endowed with the potential to become future leaders of society. The exception to this generalization is variation of treatment or provision of a remedial or compensatory kind. This is intended to enable retarded or disadvantaged children to reach a level of performance which corresponds with the average or just below average. As the variation of treatment would normally cease once this level has been reached, it is therefore consistent with the egalitarian/developmental and co-operative assumptions.

The following may be identified as variations or differentiating devices which reflect the elitist/deterministic/competitive beliefs:

1. selection for different schools (other than special schools) on criteria of performance;
2. streaming and setting;
3. specialized subject teachers (separate subjects limit the number available to all children — hence differentiating options);
4. separate subjects (rather than integrated areas with a common curriculum);
5. differently qualified teachers for different levels of 'ability';
6. compulsory homework (good performers from advantaged homes do good homework and get better: poor performers, often with uninterested parents and few facilities such as books and a quiet room do poor homework and fall further behind);
7. voluntary out-of-school activities (advantaged pupils participate more than the disadvantaged);
8. methods of. assessing, reporting, internal examining which stress success or failure and place children in rank order;
9. annual promotion dependent upon attainment;
10. prefect systems, rewarding rituals, prizes and honours awarded selectively for school work;
11. differential public examinations (the proposed GCSE may reduce the differentiation without ending it);
12. differentiated curriculum (poorer performers drop French, take European Studies, General Science, Huma-

nities, workshop subjects and work experience);
13. options in which poorer performers are discouraged
    or prevented from choosing the more rigorous sub-
    jects;
14. school uniform (used variously by pupils to demon-
    strate allegiance to school values, resentful submission
    to school coercion or total rejection of schooling).

All these differentiating devices exist in the secondary-
school system of England and Wales. All of them, except
No. 1 (different schools according to ability), can be found
in the comprehensive schools too. (Even No. 1 operates
upon 'comprehensive' schools when there are grammar
schools or any other type of selective school in the same
catchment area.) If there are comprehensive schools which
embody the ninth differentiating device (promotion by
attainment) they must be rare.

The existence of some or all of the other differentiating
devices is not generally regarded as incompatible with comprehensive philosophy; but there is a perceptible trend
towards postponing until a later age the use of these devices
which *are* adopted in the policies of a given school. There is
also a marked reduction in the total number of devices in
each comprehensive school.

Schools vary widely in the extent to which differentiation takes place. There are practical as well as philosophical
reasons why teachers (at whatever point on the philosophical
spectrum they may be placed) find that decisions are extremely difficult to take. They, like the general public, wish
to ensure the brilliant success of the outstandingly gifted.
It is widely accepted that for them segregation and special
treatment, early recognition and awards, a competitive
atmosphere, homework, specialized teachers and an academic
curriculum are likely to act as incentives and provide the
best opportunities. Teachers want success for their best
performers for the sake of the children themselves. Moreover an element in the way in which schools and individual
teachers are assessed is that of examination results and
admissions to universities. For many teachers the most
pleasurable and rewarding activity is advanced work in
depth with a class of very able pupils.

But teachers in comprehensive schools also want to raise
the standard of performance for the majority of children.

These are the pupils who, when variations of treatment are operated, are placed in lower sets or streams, are taught a more integrated curriculum, often by general rather than specialist teachers, who produce poorer homework than the high fliers, who do not rank highly in the competition for marks and who do not receive awards on Prize Day. Many teachers, whatever their educational and social philosophies, find these children very difficult to teach, and the sanctions which are available to force them to work become less effective as they reach the fourth and fifth years of the secondary schools.

For teachers who believe that ability is largely predetermined by the secondary stage and who believe in the power of competition to act as an incentive to all children, the practical problems of dealing with apathetic pupils are soluble by means of curriculum development. Considerable efforts have been made and continue to be made to devise courses which less able children will see to be relevant to their future lives. The importance of work experience for these children is emphasized. Many of these same teachers nevertheless feel that differentiation of curricula is not appropriate in the early years of the secondary schools, that different sets and streams may not be the only way to ensure that the ablest pupils reach their potential (if individualized and group work is encouraged) and that the practical problems of dealing with lower streams are best met by replacing setting or streaming by mixed-ability groups in the first and second years of the secondary school. This move has no doubt been reinforced by the practical difficulties of dividing pupils up into hierarchical sets or streams by any criteria which are fully satisfactory and are likely to be regarded as fair by pupils, parents and the teachers themselves.

It has, however, been pointed out that there is a substantial body of opinion among teachers which holds a different philosophy. They hold that potential is not sufficiently pre-determined to justify differential sets or streams or courses. They would say that pupils of secondary age are in the process of establishing an individual identity which is highly susceptible to the judgements of their attainment conveyed to them by sets, marks and reports. While these may enhance the self-esteem and efforts of those who do well in a competitive system, they present a grave danger of inducing the less successful to opt out of the race. They would claim that no one willingly competes in a race which he thinks he has no chance of winning. They discount the belief that witholding approval from poorer performers by placing them in lower sets with a different curriculum results in a redoubling of effort to obtain promotion.

For teachers who hold egalitarian/developmental/co-operative beliefs, mixed-ability grouping and the abolition of all other differentiating devices are therefore logical conclusions. But for them too practical problems arise. There are very great problems in teaching children of a wide range of performance in the same class, more in some subjects than in others. Mixed-ability teaching requires a radical change of outlook for many teachers and time for redesigning the entire course. At the age of 16, when most pupils are on the point of leaving school, there are two public examinations, GCE O-level and CSE. Courses in preparation for these examinations normally begin two years earlier (in some subjects three years are thought necessary). The more divergent the syllabuses, the more necessary it becomes to place children in different sets with different content of courses according to the examination for which they are destined. At present, therefore, even teachers who are opposed to differentiation have to accept it to some extent in the fourth and fifth years.

Opposition to the separation of GCE and CSE and the search for a common examination certainly owes its origin to the desire to reduce differentiation. Already this desire has brought about the rescinding of the pass and fail regulations of the GCE Ordinary level and replaced them by grades. In practice this change is more apparent than real, since public examinations, however they are conducted, are in themselves a most potent instrument for differentiation. Their purpose is to identify various strata of performance. The proposal of the former Secretary of State for Education, Mrs Shirley Williams, to adopt the recommendations of the Waddell Report and institute a single examination in the mid 1980s, is a compromise solution the effect of which is likely to be more cosmetic than real. It fails to meet the needs of the two very different assumptions of educationists and public alike concerning the main purposes of schooling. At one extreme, educationists opposed to differentiation on criteria of performance in school work would wish to see them abolished and replaced by a form of profile report which would be moderated for comparability. At the other extreme, many educationists see the whole purpose of schooling as progressive differentiation. For them public examinations should measure standards which are attainable by only a minority. They therefore regret the abolition of the pass/fail regulations and deplore proposals for a single examination which would embrace a wide ability range. Indeed for them an examination which no one can fail is a self-evident contradiction in terms since the purpose is to identify those who are successful. There can be no successes without failures.

The adherents of elitist/deterministic/competitive beliefs do not face difficult policy choices (though mention has been made of some practical problems). A serious dilemma, however, faces proponents of egalitarian/developmental/co-operative philosophies. They believe that differentiation gives the best chances to those who are already performing well, but that these chances are obtained by further depressing the chances of average and below-average performers. Yet they want the high success of the few as well as a raised threshold of performance for the many. Indeed all expressions of public policy as well as the pressures from parents and pupils are that schools must do both. Teachers who, in the interests (as they see it) of average and below-average pupils, wish to abandon differentiating devices (as far as public examinations will allow), have to accept that they are also abandoning the devices which encourage the success of the top-flight performers. They would probably argue that so far in our educational history we have never placed as top priority the raising of the average standard. Have we perhaps been too anxious to ensure brilliant success for the few? Would very able pupils in a more sophisticated system be perfectly capable of looking after themselves?[1]

[1] The Swedish 1962 Education Act, which set up the nine-year compulsory comprehensive school, embodies the decision to accord priority to a basic acceptable threshold of competence for all children. The Swedish Institute publication on 'Primary and Secondary Education in Sweden' describes the practical consequences of such an aim of equality of treatment. 'According to the Education Act and the syllabus guidelines, comprehensive school students shall belong to the same class to the utmost possible extent. The classes are to have the most diversified make-up possible as regards social and economic backgrounds of the students. Streaming is never practised and it is becoming less and less common to organize special remedial classes for students with difficulties at school. Other ways are sought to master such difficulties . . . Homework is assigned no more

Resources

The dilemma concerning whether to maintain differentiating devices for the sake of the gifted or to reduce them for the sake of the average and below-average child similarly affects decisions which have to be taken about the distribution of resources. In the past the balance tended to be tipped in the direction of abler performers. Grammar schools in most LEAs had better staffing ratios than secondary-modern schools. With comprehensive re-organization decisions concerning the allocation of teachers to different bands of ability became internal decisions made by heads and teachers. A more even distribution was probably common. Indeed extra staff and smaller groups of children were often provided in the remedial bands, thus tipping the balance in the other direction. Clearly this re-distribution reflects a shift of ideology. The higher grammar-school provision suggested that children who were better performers at 11 probably had higher genetic potential and were the preferred targets for national investment. The comprehensive-school investment in remedial children suggests a belief that their retardation is largely an effect of their environment, which can be remedied, and that, though they may never be brilliant, the primary task of schools is to ensure that all ordinary children achieve an acceptable level of performance.

The practical problem of resource distribution may be illustrated by examining the question of the allocation in a comprehensive school of teachers to class groups. It is important to remind ourselves that the pupil–teacher ratio in a maintained school is determined by the LEA on overall numbers of pupils and that the number of teachers available is therefore fixed each year. School policies on the use of these teachers are a matter for governors, heads and staffs. They must manage with the quota they get unless they can make a case that they are receiving unfair treatment.

than sporadically. No provision is made for leaving examinations. Although tests enter into the schoolwork no final tests are given. Final marks are awarded only in certain grades (years), chiefly at the senior level.' One might add that the common curriculum extends until the age of 13 and options in the last three years take only 10 per cent of the time. 'Out-of-school' activities called 'Freely selected work' take place in school time. It is reported (*The Guardian*, 10 April 1979) that the Swedish minority Liberal government, responding to public concern about alleged low standards, intends to introduce adjustments to the system which will encourage a return to streaming.

If one assumes an operational staffing ratio (marking and preparation periods having been allowed for) of one teacher to thirty pupils, a year group of 240 pupils should have eight teachers available

Teachers	8
Pupils	240
Ratio	1:30

It is a common practice to allocate extra teachers to pupils whose performance is retarded (remedial pupils). These extra teachers may take smaller 'remedial classes', or assist remedial pupils who are withdrawn individually or in small groups from mixed-ability classes.

If thirty remedial pupils are identified, the staffing allocation is as follows:

Teachers	2	6
Pupils	30	210
Ratio	1:15	1:35

The remedial group is staffed at the expense of the class sizes of average and gifted children (whether they are segregated in streams, sets or bands, or all together in mixed-ability groups). It has already been pointed out that the objective is one of equality rather than differentiation, since the extra staffing resources for remedial work are allocated with the intention of bringing the performance level of the remedial child up to that of the average or only marginally below average. This manoeuvre clearly results in poorer resources for the average and gifted, and may depress the lead they possess (assuming, of course, that smaller groups have the advantages claimed for them).

It has frequently been argued that 'in common justice' the extra provision made for retarded pupils should be paralleled by extra provision for the excellent performers — the 'mentally gifted' children. The deployment of staffing resources recommended would then look like this:

Teachers	2	4	2
Pupils	30	180	30
Ratio	1:15	1:45	1:15

The extra resources for the able minority must obviously
be taken from the average children. The enhancement of the
performance of the best produces a depression in the resources available to the average, and hence in their standard
of performance.[1]

It was reported (*The Times Educational Supplement*,
25 August 1978) that the Nottinghamshire LEA planned to
devote between £135,000 and £196,000 a year and twenty-
two extra teachers to a project that would ensure individual
tuition in five comprehensive schools in Beeston and Stapelford to enrich the teaching of subjects for which children
show particular brilliance. 'It is not clear how many of the
4,500 children in the Beeston and Stapelford Comprehensives
will be singled out for special teaching. One national estimate
says that 1 per cent of all school children can be classified as
very able or gifted.' The report noted that 'the area may
have been chosen because it is close to Nottingham University
and the children of academics will be attending the schools
which go comprehensive next month'. The project was the
policy of the Conservatives in the county. The Labour group
was reserving its decision because it was anxious that other
areas of education could suffer because of expenditure on the
scheme. Their spokesman on the county education committee
said, 'We do think that gifted children should have the
opportunity of achieving their potential'.

The thousands of pounds and the twenty-two extra
teachers might have been deployed to reduce class sizes
for ordinary, average children, but the Labour spokesman
does not seem to be thinking of them in stating anxiety
that other 'areas' of education could suffer. It seems that
both political parties in Nottinghamshire hold the belief
(consciously or unconsciously) that ability *is* pre-determined,
but that it may be developed in able performers though not
in average children. The emphasis is also placed firmly upon
priority for society's future leaders rather than on attempting
to raise the general level of performance.

For the five Beeston and Stapelford schools which are on
the point of 'going comprehensive' at the time of writing,

---

[1] From a deterministic standpoint it is possible to maintain that average
children are bound to remain so and that the extent of resources available for
them makes little difference. However, the assertion that extra resources will
make a difference to mentally gifted children is not logically compatible with
this deterministic belief.

the policy dilemma we have been discussing does not exist since the extra resources are coming 'ear-marked' for abler children. Even if imminent comprehensive re-organization has induced consideration of egalitarian/developmental/ co-operative policies, they are unlikely to look such a gift horse in the mouth. Had they had the freedom to deploy the extra 4.4 teachers each wherever they wished in their time-tabling, the realization that average children would be the losers would have presented them with a difficult con-undrum. As it is, it should have been a difficult conundrum for the county education committee.[1]

The theme of this chapter has been the state of con-fusion which at present surrounds some of our educational ideas. An attempt has been made to show the practical results in our schools of this confusion of thought. Such a state of uncertainty, which it has been said is the source of much of the present dissatisfaction, is in urgent need of resolution. But the choice of the educational beliefs which have been described is not easily settled by research findings. The choice between elitist or egalitarian purposes for an educational system is political, rather than practical. There is however no political consensus on this question. Con-sequently schools have to try to achieve the best balance they can by opening up the issues for discourse in meetings of governors, staff and parents. Without such discussion the formulation by a school of its aims and objectives is bound to lack firm foundations.

---

[1] A similar problem was raised by the policy of the Conservative-controlled Greater Manchester Council to set up £1.2 million education charity trust to provide 400 free or assisted places at independent schools. *The Guardian* (5 April 1979) reported that this action had been challenged in the High Court by the Labour-controlled Manchester City Council. In future years the amount required could rise to £9 million. Subsequently the High Court ruled that the Greater Manchester Council must reverse its decision. The grounds for the judge-ment were that the council concerned was not an education authority.

4 Aims and Objectives

Leadership implies conducting, guiding. These words suggest the need for a destination, or at least a direction. Teachers have always been conscious that they are engaged in a task which is intended to have an end product, and that this necessitates the existence of goals of some kind.

The goals of an entire school extend from statements about its fundamental values to the intentions of day-by-day classroom practice. They range from the most abstract, even mystical, ideals to the minutiae of a lesson plan.

The portmanteau phrase 'aims and objectives' is frequently used without a clear perception of any difference between the two component terms other than that 'aims' are considered broader and more general than 'objectives'. Alan Harris makes a useful distinction.[1] He nevertheless points out that any definitions are inevitably stipulative since the two terms do not have precise meanings in ordinary discourse.

Aims

These are expressed in comparatively general terms. They incorporate a prescription that something (such as 'growth' or 'autonomy') is worthwhile and ought to be achieved.

Objectives

These are achievements (learning, knowledge, understanding) which are capable of being expressed in less general terms than aims (e.g. understanding the nature of scientific thinking) and which are called objectives only when they are seen as necessary for the achievement of an aim.

The last statement (that the term 'objectives' is reserved for achievements which are seen to be necessary contributions to an aim) suggests that there must be a connection between

[1] Harris, A., 'Autonomy', Unit 8 in *Curriculum Philosophy and Design*, Units 6 to 8 (Jenkins, D., Pring, R., and Harris, A.), Course E283, Open University, 1972, p. 118.

the two kinds of goals. If aims are formulated first, can objectives be logically derived from them? In practice this appears to be a very difficult operation. Richard Pring points out that aims are so general that it is possible for two teachers to accept the same set of aims but to set themselves completely different sets of objectives. He explains this by saying:

> Where statements of overall aims are concerned, the goal does not seem to be some end-state that can be described and picked out and made the objective of a particular action. Rather does it appear to be a statement of certain criteria whereby you evaluate what has been done or achieved . . . Hence aims in this sense and objectives mean quite different things and it would be impossible to translate aims into a particular range of objectives.[1]

Alan Harris (op. cit.) reinforces this distinction, after pointting out that in general aims are prescriptive and evaluative while objectives are descriptive, by saying: 'In principle it should be impossible to deduce any *descriptive* statements from the *prescriptive* "Autonomy is the main aim of education".'

Does this therefore justify us in abandoning any attempt to state aims? Are aims nothing but hot air which heads of schools exhale on ceremonial occasions? That authorities of many kinds do feel the need to make general statements about the aims of education is undoubted. Pring (op. cit.) interestingly analyses the aims stated in official reports from the Hadow Report of 1926 on the Education of the Adolescent to the Plowden Report of 1967 on Children and their Primary Schools. Summarizing these aims and those stated by heads and teachers he finds that common elements include:

1. to meet the needs of the individual;
2. to meet the needs of society;
3. to foster moral development;
4. to realize an individual's potential;
5. to transmit culture;
6. to increase knowledge;
7. to develop academic excellence;
8. to encourage adaptability.

The most frequently recurring items concern 'growth', 'the needs of the individual' and 'the needs of society'.

[1] Pring, R., 'Aims and Objectives', Unit 7, in Jenkins, D., Pring, R., and Harris, A., *Curriculum Philosophy and Design*, Units 6 to 8, E283, Open University, 1972, p. 87.

Such statements are often regarded as worthless since they stipulate neither what kinds of growth are approved nor what kinds of needs, whether of individuals or of society, are to be met. They are often disappointing to those who expect aims to provide a logical basis from which objectives may be derived without further exploration of values.

Aims are nevertheless not to be despised, since they suggest the next stage to which further analysis must proceed, they provide a final yardstick by which the appropriateness of individual objectives may be judged, and they define the ultimate values held by an institution. It need come as no surprise that leaders are particularly prone to make statements of aims. They are responding to the expectations of those who have an interest in the organization which they represent. People feel a need to be informed of the philosophy of those to whom they entrust the guidance of every kind of enterprise. Writing about the leader of a very big enterprise (President Carter), James Fallows, his former chief speech-writer, complained:[1]

> I came to believe that Carter believes fifty things but no one thing. He holds explicit, thorough positions on every issue under the sun, but has no line indicating which goals (reducing unemployment? human rights?) will take precedence over which (inflation control? a SALT treaty?) when the goals conflict. Spelling out these choices makes the difference between a position and a philosophy, but it is an act foreign to Carter's mind. For certain aspects of his job . . . Carter's methods serve him well . . . but for the part of the job that involves leadership, Carter's style of thought cripples him.

If we accept the desirability of generalized aims on the grounds that, by means of the ethical position which they enshrine, they offer criteria for identifying choices between sub-aims and eventually between objectives, why do they so rarely appear to serve this purpose in practice? Eric Hoyle suggests the following explanation:

> In the past the administration of British schools has been based upon a paradox. The head has enjoyed a high degree of authority in determining the goals of the school, but has had limited influence over the classroom activities of the teacher owing to the norm of non-interference. The teacher has enjoyed a high degree of classroom autonomy, but has had relatively little involvement in changing the goals of the school.[2]

---

[1] James Fallows, 'All the President's Miens', in *The Guardian*, 24.4.79.
[2] Hoyle, E., 'Strategies of Curriculum Change' in Watkins, R. (ed.), *In-Service Training Structure and Content*, Ward Lock, 1973, p. 97.

It seems very probable that in the past the ethical positions embodied in the utterances of headmasters and headmistresses have had little impact upon classroom practice. Where there has been coincidence of values, it may often have been accidental. It will be argued in Chapter 7 on Consultation that opportunities for the whole staff group to participate in the formulation of the school's aims is an essential pre-requisite for the production of a shared commitment to them and hence for a generalized congruence between the aims and the classroom objectives. Hoyle,[1] Morris[2] and many others emphasize the element of participation as vital to the production of a climate in which change can be examined on its merits.

The concept of 'organizational health' includes 'clear goals', 'openness' and 'adequate communications'.

Among the arguments in favour of aims which are co-operatively formulated may be that such aims:

1. promote corporate responsibility;
2. safeguard against over-simplification (traditional practices are otherwise unexamined and are regarded as embodying axiomatic principles);
3. reduce oscillation and unpredictability in decision-making;
4. avoid exclusive concentration on measurable goals to the detriment of less amenable responsibilities.

It remains true that many teachers may not be enthusiastic to be involved in the discussion of aims. Some may see them as unrealistic, idealistic and bearing little, if any, relationship to classroom practice or school organization. Some will distrust aims as implying the possibility of indoctrinating or moulding pupils in accordance with a value-system which does not respect the pupils' autonomy. Of course, this would not be so if 'pupil autonomy' were the aim of the school, as suggested by Alan Harris. (op. cit.) Yet other teachers may regard the aims of education as self-evident or see the formulation of aims as a means of assessing their work and hence as a threat to their existing practice.

[1] Hoyle, E., and Bell, R., *Problems of Curriculum Innovation I*, Units 13-15, E283, Open University, 1972.
[2] Morris, Ben, 'How does a group learn to work together?' in Niblett, W. R., *How and Why Do We Learn?* Faber, 1965.

Assuming that a staff group accepts the advantages of discussing aims and discounts the grounds for resistance to the proposal, how is it possible to describe the form that such a discussion might take? Unfortunately it seems impossible to avoid a morass of abstractions by any means other than an illustration. Since there are so many ways in which aims can be expressed and since the routes by which they are reached must be individual to every staff group, an illustration may be harmful. Any illustration may appear to be prescriptive both of a particular set of goals and of the routes by which they are reached. It must therefore be stressed that the example that follows is meant to illustrate a *method* rather than a *solution*. The actual members of a group studying the question might initially be a functional group within the whole staff (the top management 'executive team' in the formal system), or a study group, or a working party, or a committee (a temporary system as described by Miles and referred to in Chapter 2). In any case their thinking would need to be shared with and debated by the entire staff in the final stages.

The group might start by selecting a very general starting point from among such aims as 'growth of the individual', the 'needs of society', or 'pupil autonomy'. Let us assume that the formula selected concerns the individual and society. Possibly this might have appealed in the form in which it is stated by Mannheim and Stewart:

> An individual is not an abstracted personality but develops as a social self in the society which exists at a certain time in history. His potentialities have to be detected as talents which may be employed in ways which are satisfying to him and to the community . . . A progressive society depends upon the development of differentiated personalities who recognise their responsibility to the community to which they belong and make their contributions as best they may with the talents which they possess.[1]

The first stage of consideration, we shall suppose, leads to the adoption of a broad aim such as 'to foster pupils' ability to contribute to the quality of life of the world of the future.' This will in turn facilitate discussion of what *attitudes* pupils will require to induce them to want to make such a contribution (readiness to be of service to others, confidence in their own power to make a contribution).

[1] Mannheim, K., and Stewart, W. A. C., *An Introduction to the Sociology of Education*, Routledge & Kegan Paul, 1962, p. 49.

It will also lead to a consideration of the kinds of *know-ledge and skills* which are likely to be needed in the world during the pupils' lifetime. It would also probably be pointed out that *opportunities* to utilize their skills and knowledge fully may be denied to pupils who are not afforded the qualifications or the guidance appropriate to their skills and knowledge. Thus a series of sub-aims might emerge from discussion by the staff group engaged on this task. Each of these sub-aims may be considered with a view to drawing out its implications, in the setting of the individual school concerned, for decisions concerning the curriculum, the organization, the resources and the disciplinary system. The policies which ensue do not necessarily follow by reasonable inference from the aims or sub-aims: different teachers, either as individuals or as a group, may select different policies as appropriate means towards the aims identified. While most teachers, for instance, might see the safeguarding of public and private property as bound up with the promotion of pupils' confidence and sense of security (and hence as a legitimate aim), the rigidity of control which some would deem desirable might appear unnecessarily restrictive to others. Some might see confidence as enhanced by mixed-ability teaching, while others would regard a streamed organization as providing a greater sense of security. One policy might be suitable in the conditions of a particular school and another in different conditions.

Each sub-aim can be defined in such a way as to open up school policies to examination and pave the way for concrete decisions. Thus:

1. *Confidence: To provide experiences for pupils which demonstrate their individual value to the school community.* Policies regarding pupil grouping, independent work and private study, choice in the curriculum, prefectship or voluntary leadership opportunities, encouragement and commendation, clubs and societies, experience of success, modes of address, sanctions and punishment methods, measures to prevent bullying, counselling facilities, remedial help policies, staff development policy, pupil consultation, storage of

property, lost property, first aid, care of the sick, and so on.

2. *Service*   *To enable pupils to experience the satisfaction of unselfish service in school and the community beyond.* Community service schemes, organization of response to charity appeals, liaison with local institutions, encouragement to join voluntary service organizations, curriculum content regarding the third world, the needs and feelings of others, monitorial or representational appointments of pupils by pupils for offices of service to pupils (library, school book-shops, tuck-shops, refreshments, etc.).

3. *Opportunity*   *To make accessible to pupils information, skills and qualifications which will enable them to select and undertake an adult role in society.* Examinations, careers education, careers information for parents and pupils, help with self-appraisal, experience in making decisions, preparation for applications and interviews, non-examination forms of 'qualifications' — athletic, Duke of Edinburgh award, music, leaving certificates, or references for potential employers and higher or further education, etc.

4. *Skills and Knowledge*   *To facilitate growth in all the modes of human understanding* (or in all the skills and knowledge the individual needs or society needs, or whatever may be the conceptual framework adopted for curriculum design). This is likely to prove the most difficult area in which decisions have to be made since it is clearly impossible to initiate children into *all* knowledge and *all* skills. An analysis of the literature on the curriculum will suggest ways in which to approach the discussion of the subject. It seems likely that many staff groups would select for emphasis:

(a) literacy, (b) numeracy, (c) scientific understanding, (d) creative and aesthetic experiences, (e) social and environmental studies, (f) physical and recreational skills, (g) the development of an individual code of moral and spiritual values.

Innumerable further questions must also be explored: What foreign languages should be taught and to whom? Are the 'areas' mentioned in the preceding paragraph the only or the most appropriate way of dividing up knowledge? What part do traditional 'subjects' play in the way we present knowledge? How much 'integration' is appropriate? What is the extent of pupil choice which should be provided for, and at what stages of the secondary-school course? What specific skills needed by pupils are not necessarily implicit features of any of the 'areas' which have been designated (whatever these may be)? When these have been identified, do we agree to distribute separate packages of skills and knowledge to the 'most likely' department for their exclusive attention, or do we distribute responsibility for attending to them to all departments, thus instituting 'whole-school policies' for skills in learning, reading, health and hygiene, 'graphicity', entry to employment, personal relationships, money management, racial understanding and many others?

In this last sub-aim concerning the nature of the knowledge and skills which a staff group considers the school should try to impart (and possibly under the previous headings of sub-aims also), we already appear to have entered the field of detailing objectives if we follow Alan Harris's definition quoted at the opening of this chapter. If we continue to follow this style of classification, more detailed goals at the classroom level (explored by teams of teachers, departments or faculties and designed to relate the aims to specific tasks) might be termed sub-objectives.

On the other hand, in much of the literature about educational (or instructional) objectives, the term 'objectives' is frequently qualified by the word 'behavioural'.[1] The advocates of behavioural objectives often appear to imply that no goals should be called objectives unless they:

1. Describe *student* rather than *teacher* behaviour;
2. State the *product* of the operation rather than the *process*;
3. State *terminal* behaviour rather than *subject-matter*;
4. Concentrate on a single learning outcome.

It is comforting therefore to note that Kibler concedes that not all objectives can be stated in these terms:

> As a matter of fact, it seems that the more significant an objective is, the more difficult it is to measure. Examples of objectives which fall into the difficult-to-specify-and-measure category are those in the areas of problem-solving, creativity, attitudes and values. The only solution we see to this problem is for such objectives to be specified as clearly as possible and for the instructor to be as resourceful as he can in developing evaluative measures, including attitude inventories and creativity tests.[2]

It is clear that, as Alan Harris states in the work quoted at the beginning of this chapter, any distinction between 'aims' and 'objectives' must be stipulative. For convenience it seems sensible to adopt the term 'aim' for goals which are generalized, prescriptive and contain obvious value-judgements. The term 'objective' can then be used to apply to more limited and specific goals which are predominantly descriptive of learning outcomes.

In drawing up the objectives of a course or a unit within a course, it is important that we should not overlook or discard those objectives in the categories mentioned by Kibler which appear to resist clear specification and measurement. It is equally important that we take care to specify as accurately as possible, for goals where it is appropriate, the pupil performance which we are seeking to achieve by the work which we plan. Specific learning outcomes

[1] Gronlund, N. E., *Stating Behavioural Objectives for Classroom Instruction*, Macmillan, 1970.
Mager, R. F., *Preparing Instructional Objectives*, Fearon, 1975.
Tanner, D., *Using Behavioural Objectives in the Classroom*, Macmillan, 1972.
[2] Kibler, R., Barker, L., Miles, D., *Behavioural Objectives and Instruction*, Allyn and Bacon, 1970, p. 5.

may be listed as examples of a general instructional objective. Gronlund (op. cit.) gives examples of which the following are typical:

Uses critical thinking skills in reading
1. distinguishes between facts and opinions;
2. distinguishes between facts and inferences;
3. identifies cause−effect relations;
4. identifies errors in reasoning;
5. distinguishes between relevant and irrelevant arguments;
6. distinguishes between warranted and unwarranted generalizations;
7. formulates valid conclusions from written material;
8. specifies assumptions needed to make conclusions true.

Teachers trying to state their objectives whether in behavioural terms or not, will find the taxonomies of interest.[1] These classify all the learning outcomes that can be thought of in major categories, with specific examples of pupil behaviour within each category. The categories are arranged in ascending order from the simplest to the most complex. General objectives are stated and are illustrated by lists of pupils' actions (for example, defines, describes, infers, predicts, discriminates, distinguishes, combines, relates, contrasts, interprets, and so on), which are useful not only for formulating objectives but also for testing, evaluating and reporting pupil performance.

Perhaps this last reference to the taxonomies and to instructional and behavioural objectives might lead us to regard objectives as related entirely to the goals of the formal curriculum and the learning experiences which are time-tabled. For this reason it may be as well to recall that children (and adults as well) are learning something, good or bad, desirable or undesirable, the whole time, whether they are in class or out of it; indeed whether they are in school or out of it. The things they learn at school from every aspect of its life are the school's responsibility. Many of these influences are the result of decisions made for reasons other than educational ones, such as administrative convenience or

---

[1] Bloom, B. S. (ed.) *et al., Taxonomy of Educational Objectives: Cognitive Domain,* David McKay Co., 1956.

Krathwohl, D. R., *et al., Taxonomy of Educational Objectives: Affective Domain,* David McKay Co., 1964.

Simpson, E., *The Classification of Educational Objectives: Psychomotor Domain,* Urbana, 1966.

financial economy. Because their educational significance may be overlooked, the impact of such decisions is often called the 'hidden curriculum'. Whatever goals are accepted for the instructional curriculum should be the criteria by which school policies as a whole are judged. Decisions about pupil grouping, the serving of school dinners, accessibility of classrooms, libraries and other facilities, consultative pupil councils, modes of address between staff and pupils, the school rules, and so on *ad infinitum*, may have important effects upon pupils' attitudes. Although the school's aims may be consciously pursued through the official learning programme, many of them can also be approached through the daily routine of school life. In a coherent school, the hidden curriculum and the instructional programmes will reinforce each other.

The emphasis upon the pre-specification of objectives in all educational planning seems to be most marked in the United States of America and, along with other forms of innovation, no doubt owed its genesis to the threat to national survival which appeared to be presented by the launching of Sputnik 1 by the Russians in 1957. The economic situation of the United Kingdom in the 1970s seemed to be laying less emphasis on innovation and to be replacing it by accountability and 'a return to standards'. Accountability, no less than innovation, requires clear statements of aims and objectives. The government initiative to encourage schools to pay attention to this requirement was launched by the then Prime Minister, Mr James Callaghan, in his Ruskin Speech on 22 October 1976. 'The goals of our education, from nursery school through to adult education, are clear enough. They are to equip children to the best of their ability for a lively, constructive place in society and also fit them to do a job of work.'

This preliminary statement was followed by the 'Great Debate' on education and the publication of the 'Green Paper' in July 1977.[1] This paper listed the eight aims of the schools as the Department of Education and Science saw them. These aims were statements of the issues raised by the series of regional conferences addressed by Mrs Shirley Williams, then Secretary of State for Education and Science. Such statements were not meant to be more than guidelines

[1] DES, *Education in Schools: a consultative document* Cmnd 6869, HMSO, 1977.

designed to stimulate schools to take a hard look at the curriculum and devise their own statements of aims and objectives. Indeed the Green Paper states that its proposals 'may be built upon, altered in the course of discussion and superseded by developments which may occur.' In reviewing the aims of their own schools, teachers might well take the Green Paper's eight aims as their starting point. Many may well feel that the eight aims require some co-ordinating principle in the form of a more general initial statement, since the selection made lacks coherence as well as presenting an appearance of incompleteness by omitting any reference to physical development and preparation for parenthood and family life. The Green Paper's eight aims are pitched at the level of 'sub-aims' and require extension both 'upwards' to the level of greater generalization and 'downwards' to the level of more specific objectives.

Reference to 'teachers' or 'groups of teachers' as those most likely to be engaged in drawing up statements of aims and objectives is not meant in this context to exclude the participation of other interests outside the school, but rather to highlight the opinion that the initiative in this task is likely to rest with the professional element within the school. The role of the headmaster or headmistress as initiator and stimulus in relation to the teaching staff, and as a bridge (not the sole one but a vital one) between the school and its governors, parents and the wider local community must be considered crucial in this matter. Recommendation No. 37 of the Taylor Report specifies aims and objectives as a responsibility of the governing body.

> The governing body should be given by the LEA the responsibility for setting the aims of the school, for considering the means by which they are pursued, for keeping under review the school's progress towards them, and for deciding upon action to facilitate such progress.[1]

The formulation of aims and objectives is bound to be a time-consuming task and teachers may feel tempted to postpone it. As long as it is tackled on a long-term basis so that the essential responsibility for maintaining day-to-day functioning is not handicapped, it is nevertheless a project well worth while undertaking. Teachers have accepted and indeed often welcomed such concepts as staff development

[1] DES, *A New Partnership for Our Schools*, HMSO, 1977.

and regular, organized self-appraisal, school evaluation, accountability, staff participation in decision-making and improved procedures for reports and assessment of pupil performance. All of these developments are closely linked with greater shared awareness of a school's aims and objectives. These also form a basis for re-examining the staff structure of responsibilities and the roles fulfilled by teachers in that structure. It is hoped that the connection will be apparent when these subjects are discussed in the following chapters.

5 Roles

Attitudes towards any discussion of 'roles' are often coloured by the associations of the word with acting and the theatre. In origin the word appears to derive from the parchment roll upon which an actor's part was written. Since actors assume roles temporarily, apparently by submerging their own personality and adopting that of an imagined, fictitious character, people who value integrity and 'natural, honest behaviour' in social and professional relationships are sometimes suspicious of any reference to roles. 'Playing' or 'adopting' or 'assuming' a role suggests artificiality and deception. It may be accepted that such deception in the theatre has its own integrity since audiences themselves recognize that drama is an activity involving the willing suspension of their disbelief.

In education, deception is not acceptable. Roles in institutions and in society are not therefore the same as theatrical roles. Deriving from the theatrical origins of the word, we nevertheless speak of the *'parts* different people *play'* in society. In this context, however, we are referring to tasks and responsibilities undertaken by groups or individuals on behalf of others. Normally the individual personality of the role-holder is fully engaged in these tasks rather than being laid aside. There is a degree of permanence and continuity which is not a characteristic of the acting role. In this chapter we shall not refer to *parts* or to *playing* roles but to fulfilling or discharging roles.

In essence, then, a role is a set of tasks or responsibilities; and the personality of the role-holder is a strongly determining influence upon the way in which these responsibilities are fulfilled. There is another influence which is generally referred to as 'role expectations'. The phrase is used to refer both to the nature and objectives of the responsibilities and how they will be fulfilled, and also to describe a pattern of

behavioural characteristics which may be peripheral to the
task itself. There is wide recognition of the importance of
clarifying the role expectations which refer to the nature and
objectives of responsibilities. If a superior expects a certain
job to be done but has not conveyed this fact to a subordinate,
organizational effectiveness is lost. There is now much more
emphasis in most types of enterprise upon role specification,
which aims to describe expectations about tasks and the
manner of discharging them.

Although expectations about general patterns of behaviour
are rarely explicitly stated, they may have powerful consequences, as is demonstrated by the forced resignation of a
comprehensive school headmistress on the grounds that she
was pregnant and unmarried. Expectations of what society
regards as exemplary moral behaviour are in practice conditions of employment for a headmistress. Expectations of
diametrically opposite behaviour for show-business and
television personalities may be deduced from the general
approval or tolerance which greets similar conduct from
them. Since compliance with these unwritten expectations
produces approval or rejection of the role-holder, most
people conform to them and the behaviour expected becomes
not only a feature of their conduct but even of their attitudes
and patterns of thought. Thus role expectations interact
with personalities to mould and modify them.

Perhaps the role expectations concerning the marital
status of headmistresses who are pregnant may have a rational
connection with the role they fulfil as exemplars to the
young. (In practice the extent to which young people model
their behaviour upon that of pop stars rather than headmistresses is unresearched.) Although some behavioural
expectations may be logically connected with the contemporary responsibilities of roles, many such expectations
are no longer so connected and are out of date. Such expectations may be called 'stereotypes' when the disparity or
irrelevance is not clearly perceived and 'caricatures' when
the disparity or irrelevance is recognized.

Education abounds in stereotypes, from the professor
who is expected to be absent-minded to the 'D stream'
pupil who is expected to be a 'thickie'. The 'image' of the
art teacher contains features of either paint-stained smocks
or slightly eccentric colourful dress. Mathematics teachers
in the abstract are perceived as quantifiers to whom nothing

is valid if it cannot be measured. They lack human sympathy. Headmasters have loud voices and an assertive, dogmatic, manner. The strange thing is that in a very generalized way these images are so often confirmed — strange because human personality is so varied, there are so many variables too in the circumstances of the life and work of each of these stereotyped roles, and because the characteristics identified are by no means essential to the satisfactory performance of the role. The most probable explanation is that the role-holders themselves are so often reminded by other people of what is expected of them that they minister to their own need to establish a clear identity by responding consciously or unconsciously to these expectations.

When it comes to expectations which are irrelevant to role performance and even inhibit desirable changes in the fulfilment of a role, the attitude which attributes role-associated characteristics to pre-determined personality traits will be unhelpful. This attitude assumes that the observed characteristics of art teachers, mathematics teachers, headmasters and D stream pupils existed before their adoption of the role concerned. Furthermore, these characteristics are taken to account for their adoption of the role concerned. If this is the assumption, no change in expectations is likely to be considered because expectations are seen as consequences rather than causes. An attitude which assumes that many characteristics are environmentally determined will lead to reappraisal of expectations and may free the role-holder, enabling him or her to adopt characteristics which are relevant to the responsibilities of the role concerned.

In considering the roles fulfilled by people in schools, we shall apply the open-systems hypothesis described in the second chapter and also the related theory of the nature of leadership.

Pupils

The children who attend school have a primary task. Like the 'enterprise' described by A. K. Rice, pupils make 'imports' of information and experiences which the school presents. They 'convert' this material into attitudes, concepts and skills and they make 'exports' of written and oral responses, workshop, cookery and art-room products, physical movements, music, experimental results and many other forms of behaviour. The part of them (the will?) which decides whether to attend or to day-dream, whether to work or to laze, whether to answer or to remain silent, fulfils the leadership function in each individual. Though teachers can and do provide encouragement to make the first response in each pair and discouragement against the second, the pupil is an autonomous task system and the final decision (which is always the responsibility of leadership) lies on the import/conversion/export twin boundaries of himself. The process of learning represented by this model of the individual pupil as a self-contained task system is a natural one, which may well have been developed by the processes of evolution. If survival is a universal basic instinct, learning is the means of achieving it. Providing therefore that the connection between learning something and personal advantage is clearly perceived, we should expect that children want to learn.

If children have presented to them this image of the pupil role — one which identifies it as co-operating with teachers in an active primary task of learning and that human satisfactions derive from task performance — we shall provide the expectations which encourage children to respond in this way. Experienced teachers know that those who behave as if it never crosses their mind that children might be unco-operative usually have co-operative classes. Teachers who constantly expect misbehaviour and threaten children with punishment if they misbehave usually have to carry out their threats.

Teachers

As subject teachers, they are in charge of classes. As form tutors, they are responsible for tutor groups. The class or group is a task system where time, space, equipment and materials are brought together in order to achieve the objective of acquiring a pre-planned selection of skills, knowledge and attitudes, The teacher is the leader or manager of this enterprise. The general objectives are determined in advance as falling within the limits of school policy and departmental or pastoral planning; but the teacher has the responsibility of selecting the goals of an individual lesson and the methods he or she will use. Interpreted in the terms of the open-systems theory, the leadership of the teacher must be directed towards decisions concerning the 'imports' (the materials, equipment and ideas to be introduced), the 'conversion' (the manner in which these materials will be used to effect the desired learning), and the 'exports' (the nature of the response or output to be called for from the pupils).

Although in one sense, a teacher inside his classroom is in sole charge of what then happens and is free — within the limits of the reactions of his pupils — to order the lesson as he wishes, in fact the exercise of freedom is limited by the policies of his or her department and those of the school. A number of factors place great limitations upon the teacher's autonomy, and the price of ignoring them is severe for his pupils as well as his colleagues. Some factors concern the 'input' and 'conversion' (the ability and the previous experience of the pupils, the books and materials available, the length of the lesson, the room and its furniture, the departmental syllabuses, the approaches to which children are accustomed in other lessons, school policies regarding homework, marking, the way pupils are normally addressed, and many others). Other factors concern the nature of the 'output' required, which has to meet the needs of society, the views of parents, the demands of the syllabus to be covered the following term or year, and the requirements of internal and public examinations. All the decisions which teachers have to make as classroom managers must be related to the environment of that classroom. No enterprise can be successfully conducted without a constant eye being kept on the input which comes from outside and the output which goes outside.

As no human being can foretell every reaction or eventuality in a set of relationships involving more than thirty people, no amount of preliminary planning can ensure that a teacher avoids the necessity to make minute-by-minute decisions on the intangible boundary of the class about what to admit as contributory to the learning task and what to bar. The teacher's personal appearance, dress, language and manner are important details which children may learn to imitate. The teacher himself is an element in the resources of the task-system of the class. Society therefore has a right to attach to the teaching role certain expectations which are related to what is deemed desirable for children to imitate. A teacher who says 'As long as I teach them conscientiously, it does not matter how I dress' has too narrow a view of the teacher's role. On the other hand, difficult though it is, because it is largely unconscious, teachers should obviously resist conformity with irrelevant and unconstructive stereotypes of the teacher's role which present him or her as pedantic, sarcastic, authoritarian, ingenuous and inexperienced in the ways of the rough, harsh world outside school. Besides being leaders of their own sub-systems (the classes or tutor groups) all teachers are also members of the full management team of the whole school. The responsibilities attached to this latter role are discussed in Chapter 7.

Middle managers (department/faculty, house/year heads)

The task of middle managers is to provide leadership to teams of class or tutor-group managers. For the first part of this section the term 'department' will be used for convenience to cover faculties as well as pastoral units (house or year). If discussion about objectives and syllabuses appears inappropriate to pastoral units, it is because the latter have too often been regarded as having no learning objectives. It is the argument of a later chapter on pastoral and curricular sub-systems that both serve the purpose of pupil learning, only differing in the composition of the pupil groupings and the nature of the learning objectives.

Middle managers, like all leaders except those at the summit or at the base of an extended hierarchy, have a dual role. They are both members of a higher-echelon management body and leaders of their own sub-systems. As members of a general management team they contribute their particular skills and expertise to questions concerning the whole institution (such as the general aims of the school). As managers of their own sub-systems they provide the members of their groups with the leadership required for the effective internal organization of the sub-system concerned.

The leadership of middle managers in the first place consists in gaining the commitment of the members of his group to a set of clearly understood objectives. He or she may exercise this leadership in a variety of ways which will be further explored in Chapter 7 on Participation and Consultation. The mode of leadership, to be effective, should be consistent with the one normally exercised in the institution by other levels in the structure and by other middle managers at the same level. All teachers are members simultaneously of a number of different task groups. Management exercised by any of the recognized modes, if consistent, is likely to be more effective than if it is fluctuating and unpredictable. The drawing up of objectives must be the first task; and ensuring that they are understood and will be pursued by the whole team of teachers is the second. Once objectives have been defined for the whole course there is a tendency to assume that the task is finished for an indefinite period into the future. It is in itself such a long and complex job. Nevertheless the good middle manager will keep a copy of the department's objectives in a loose-leaf file and always open on his or her desk so that notes can be made and questions raised about items which were unsatisfactory. Syllabus objectives and methods must be open to continuous reappraisal.

The head of a large department is responsible for all the work of all the teachers in the department and all the classes which he or she has delegated to them. In a school of 1,000 pupils a mathematics head of department may be responsible for 8,000 mathematics lessons each year. All these 8,000 lessons have to be related to each other and to the environment of the department consisting of the work going on in the rest of the school. It is probable that in the past heads of department have been better at co-ordinating the work in their own subject than at co-ordinating it with what went on elsewhere. Subject departments are so often castles surrounded by a moat that teachers sometimes forget that the inhabitants of the castles move regularly from one to another every time the bell rings. One small piece of research revealed that 12-year-old pupils in a certain school were 'doing' coal mines in the same year simultaneously in science, geography and history. There was no co-ordination between any two classes about how the topic was treated. Only the pupils knew until the enquiry revealed the information. They made no comment!

The task of a head of department is, then, to relate to each other all the task systems which are classes and the elements of which each is composed and to relate the whole to the environment of the department (Fig. 1). The elements in each class are the teachers, the pupils, the time available, the space in which the work is performed, the ideas (facts, concepts, skills, attitudes) which are to be learned by pupils and the ideas about how they can most effectively learn them, the equipment to be used to bring about this learning,

Fig. 1   The management of a department

The task is to relate the elements together and
to the environment

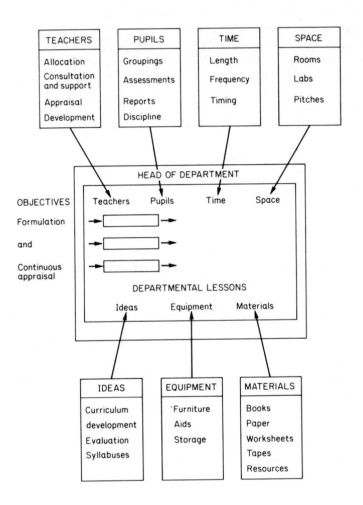

and the materials acquired or prepared which are to be the
basis of the pupils' work. In connection with all these elements the head of department's task is to select, acquire,
make accessible. In all these spheres he or she will have two
overriding considerations constantly in mind: first, fostering
the skills and developing the effectiveness of the teachers

concerned so that their management of their classes may be enhanced, second, seeking information about what other departments are doing and informing them of what his or her department is doing.

In the light of this wide and heavy responsibility it is possible to list the qualities most likely to help the head of department fulfil it.

1. *Contribution* as a middle manager to the formulation of school goals.
2. *A sense of purpose*: commitment to school goals and clarification of departmental objectives.
3. *Confidence* in self and in subordinate colleagues.
4. *Unselfishness*: readiness to share by delegation.
5. *Openness and availability*: communication with departmental colleagues, other staff, pupils, parents, head, primary schools, governors, advisers and inspectors.
6. *A sense of interdependence*: readiness to co-operate with other departments; support, encouragement, advice, appropriate action to help subordinate colleagues; staff development and instigation of in-service training.
7. *Awareness of role*: recognition of all aspects of the task, readiness to discharge it without status consciousness.
8. *Judgement*: ability to appraise the work of subordinate colleagues in a helpful way so that intervention presents an opportunity rather than a threat.
9. *Broad interests* in the work of other departments.
10. *Resolution, decisiveness*: establishing policies and explaining reasons for them.
11. *Personal teaching skills*: effectiveness as a teacher of all ages and abilities of pupils as a means of providing an example for imitation by junior teachers.
12. *Orderliness and method*: in storage and listing of books and apparatus and in keeping accounts and records.

In discussing, in a later chapter, the essential similarity and minor differences between the pastoral and curricular sub-systems, reference will be made to the images which each creates. The common theory is that curricular departments are to do with teaching and learning and that house or year groups are to do with caring and social activities. As a result middle managers in the pastoral system are in danger of being stereotyped as soft-hearted, or even as 'soft'. By contrast heads of subject departments may be saddled with the image of being tough or hard. This kind of polarization is echoed in the supposed division between affective and cognitive education, child-centredness and subject-centredness, and even within the curricular area, between rigorous 'disciplines' like mathematics and physics, and soft options like art, literature and biology. Such mythological oversimplifications bear little if any relationship to the truth. In fact softness and hardness are inseparable opposite faces of each coin. Since pastoral teachers are as much responsible for discipline as curricular teachers, and mathematics teachers are as much concerned with their pupils as people as are art teachers, the images are plainly not reflections of the facts. Nevertheless the idea that pastoral heads are experts in understanding children and in providing them with recreational activities is not easily dismissed unless a more plausible reason for their existence can be found. This question is pursued in Chapter 6. At this point the intention is limited to indicating that the separation of the roles of departmental and house or year heads along the dimension of caring and demanding presents a danger to both as limiting their roles as teachers responsible for both.

Senior teachers

Larger schools have available two or three posts at a salary scale above that of heads of department and pastoral heads and below that of deputy heads. As they are relative newcomers on the Burnham scene, there was at first some uncertainty about what use schools should make of these appointments. Two solutions were adopted initially: the first was to select two or three of the biggest departments (often mathematics, English and science) and promote the heads of those departments from scale 4 to senior-teacher scale. This solution was not always very acceptable in schools where a faculty system existed. A head of 'humanities' or 'creative studies' might be responsible for more subjects, teachers and materials than one of the more monolithic faculties. The second solution advocated by a number of educationists was to use senior-teacher scales to raise the remuneration of certain outstandingly competent teachers outside the formal structure of responsibility and without relation to it.

This latter proposal is in need of careful examination. Behind the idea lie three beliefs:

1. that there are good teachers who have refused promotion in the formal structure because they have teaching skills which would not be utilized in a promoted post;
2. that such teaching skills are so rare that those who possess them should be encouraged to devote themselves to using them to the exclusion of all other work;
3. that the level of promoted posts in the formal structure is in direct ratio to an increase in 'administrative' work, which has only a remote relationship with teaching.

There may well be 'good' teachers who have refused promotion and even some who have done so because they think that once promoted they would have fewer opportunities to use their skills. In some schools, perhaps, they have been encouraged to think of teaching and learning as taking place only with children, in school subjects. A competent teacher should be encouraged to teach other teachers how to teach. The formal structure of responsibility ought to offer ample opportunities for the holder of a recognized post to be doing this. Staff development must be acknowledged to be an important function of a head of department. The talents and experience of a really outstanding teacher make him or her an appropriate person to be appointed Professional Tutor on a senior-teacher or deputy-head scale. It seems a curiously defeatist attitude which would acquiesce in the idea that the influence of a 'good teacher' (however this may be defined) should be confined to the limited number of classes he or she can teach personally rather than being more widely disseminated throughout the whole staff. Encouragement is often given to the notion that some people have innate qualities of being 'good with children' but are inept with adults. Indeed this is often the public's view of all teachers as 'men among boys and boys among men'. No school should collude with such a theory. If some teachers are 'good with children', they should be given every opportunity and encouragement to become 'good' with adults also, if they are not already.

In the suggestion that senior-teacher scales should be used to reward good teachers for 'staying in the classroom'

there may lurk a further conviction that good teachers are
born, not made, and that the skills they have cannot be
imparted to others because they are intuitive. Such a belief
is deeply entrenched in some views about teaching. It may
be related to the view that personality is static and cannot
be developed once one has reached maturity. It is only
comparatively recently that the DES has accepted the
principle that all aspiring teachers – even graduates – need
initial training. (The current exception made for mathematicians and scientists is merely an acknowledgement of market
forces and does not affect the principle.) The present emphasis is upon in-service education and training and upon school-
based staff development. If we do not use our good teachers
in this work we are neglecting the most valuable resource
we possess. Senior-teacher scales are a valuable way of
providing the opportunity and the reward for the work of
making bad teachers into average ones and average ones into
good ones. We must be clear though that the work that is
being recognized is staff development, not remaining 'in the
classroom'.

The second belief underlying the suggestion that senior-
teacher scales should be a reward for remaining in the classroom is a fear, akin to panic in some quarters, that good
teachers are extremely rare. The proposal that all good teachers
receive senior-teacher scales suggests that there would be only
two or three in each large school and none in small schools.

The general level of performance may not be brilliant,
but it is not so frighteningly low that the best of them
should be paid extra to spend all their time with children
to the exclusion of work to help their colleagues to improve.
Such a policy would be to despair of raising the general level
or to hand the work of in-service training over to people
outside the school. The logical development of paying the
best teachers to remain full time in the classroom would be
that the training responsibilities of heads of departments
(usually paid below senior-teacher scales) would be in the
hands of the second best rather than the best.

The third belief, that promoted posts entail an increased
load of 'administrative' work which is distinct from the
responsibility of teaching, deserves very serious consideration. There is widespread unease that the better one is as a
teacher the more likely one is to be promoted 'out of teaching
into administration'. Thus the pupils lose the benefit of

being taught by the best teachers and the teachers themselves
are deprived of the activity which they do best and which
they therefore, presumably, most enjoy. This anxiety, which
is so often expressed by educationists both inside and outside the schools, arises from the fact that a greater number
of teachers than hitherto are now involved in the more
complex management of large comprehensive schools. In
order to fulfil their management responsibilities, they usually
receive a lighter teaching time-table in the new conditions.
They may teach only half-time or three-quarters time compared with teachers who have no responsibilities in middle
or top management.

The appearance is created of more teachers being taken
out of teaching and being engaged in 'administration'. This
is in fact largely an illusion, since an eight-form entry comprehensive is the same size as four two-form entry schools,
all of which have heads and deputy heads with reduced
teaching time-tables.

When people use the word 'administration' in this context and deplore the involvement of experienced teachers
in it, they appear to assume that it is an activity which is
strongly contrasted with and different from the activity of
teaching. Asked to define 'administration' they would
probably say it concerns processing paper for some unknown
and unprofitable bureaucratic purpose which has nothing to
do with the children's learning. Administrative tasks are
usually considered to be tedious, menial, repetitive and
unproductive. If this is what administration is then it has no
place at all in schools, whoever performs it. Certainly no
teacher (or clerical staff either) should be expected to fill
in forms, make returns, write letters or pass around any
papers which have no relationship with children's learning
and which merely serve to keep someone in employment.
(It is an important task of educational management to relate
all paperwork to teaching and learning and to abolish any
which is not so related.)

No teacher's responsibilities should be confined exclusively
to menial, routine tasks, even when it can be shown that
these are clearly essential to teaching and learning. That there
are tedious chores involved in every role, however creative,
cannot be denied; but they should be the servants, not the
masters, of any professional responsibility.

Teachers at all levels are managers. The classroom teacher's lesson notes and records are essential 'administrative' ingredients in his management of a class. So it is not true that only promotion brings administration in its train. Nor is it true that it must (much less should) take up a greater proportion of the time of a promoted teacher than of a junior one. The origin of the view that administration concerns a tangle of ill-conceived maintenance chores probably lies in the kind of activities allotted by heads to deputy heads and senior masters or mistresses in the early days of comprehensive reorganization. Heads who in smaller schools had previously enjoyed personal control over the creative aspects of management were unsure how to delegate without losing control. Control appeared inseparable from accountability. This question is examined in more detail in the later pages of this chapter, which discuss the roles of deputy heads and senior masters and mistresses.

Either there should be no 'administration' (if it is as dull and useless as some people think) or 'administration' is the same as 'management'. In schools, 'management' is the management of learning, and this is a fit and proper role for an experienced teacher. The management task in schools concerns the leadership of other teachers in developing their effectiveness and is therefore a natural extension of that commitment to growth and learning which, presumably, first inspired the young teacher to embark upon an educational career. Teaching is not solely instruction, nor is it only concerned with the young in classrooms. Teaching is educational management at a variety of different levels.

Those who bemoan the promotion of good teachers to become administrators should be obliged to define their terms. They create confusion and guilt in those who accept promotion; they may deter some able teachers from contributing as much as they should to management; and they even obscure the aims and purposes of teachers in senior posts.

Deputy heads and senior masters and mistresses

The leadership of complex institutions must be at all times available and specified, since immediate short-term and long-term decisions may be required at any time. It has been pointed out that all leadership is concerned with relating the internal processes of an institution to its environment. Heads of schools are therefore responsible for importing knowledge and ideas from beyond the walls of the school, for exporting information about it and also for conducting its internal life. When the duties of heads take them away from the school buildings there is an obvious need for a substitute to act on their behalf. He or she must be committed to the same purposes and policies, aware of current moves and problems and be an effective competent senior member of the institution whose opinions and decisions command general respect. Provision is made in teachers' salary scales for this responsibility of substituting by the creation of one or two (or three) deputy-head posts.

The nature of the deputy-head post has always posed management problems. The actual task of substituting for the head who is absent from the school or not available in the school takes up only a minority of the deputy's time. How is he or she occupied during the balance of time? In the single-order, small school the deputy could be a class teacher like everyone else. In the complex school with differentiation into second- and even third-order systems (these are discussed in Chapter 6), each with its own management, a deputy head could hardly be a class teacher on a lower level of management than middle managers if this was his/her sole function other than substituting. Nor would it be satisfactory that he or she should hold a middle-management post, as this would be too closely identified with one part of the school's total task. A role associated with a subject or with a selected age-range or a 'vertical' section of the pupils would appear to contradict the deputy's need to have wider authority in the activities of the school. The deputy's main need is to be closely associated with the top management.

In the early years of comprehensive reorganization heads found themselves overwhelmed by a massive increase in responsibilities and tasks, many of them creative and imaginative and many routine and implementational. Their accountability to others made them reluctant to delegate the creative and imaginative responsibilities. This reluctance may have stemmed partly from the satisfactions which derive from such responsibilities. Partly also, other teachers and the public in general expected heads to set their personal stamp upon new institutions and were unready to see such work delegated to 'assistant' staff, even deputies. Heads recognized the need to delegate something. Both the limitations of their own time and the need to involve deputies in top management urged delegation. The routine, implementational tasks were those most frequently delegated, those often called administration', which involved no initiative on the part of the deputy and were therefore 'safe', in the sense that the head retained direct personal control over all fundamental change. The solution which was frequently found was to construct for the deputy the new role of 'personal assistant' to the head. Now personal assistants are not unknown in industry and commerce, but the role-holders are normally junior members of an executive team and lack authority.

Notices in the press advertising vacancies for deputy heads still sometimes refer to the duties involved as 'the usual responsibilities of deputies'. If 'further details' are promised to enquirers these can take the form of a list of implementational tasks, which include:

daily checking of class registers;
notification of absent and unpunctual pupils;
daily cover for absent staff members;
preparation of time-table data;
examination time-tables;
arbitration between pupil and teacher in cases of indiscipline;
the school calendar of events;
staff representation on the Parent/Teacher Association Committee;
sick children and first aid for injuries;
programmes for visitors to the school;
supervision of audio-visual aids;
notification of breakages and arrangements for repairs;
lost property;
supervision of toilets;
duty rosters;
pupils' dress, appearance and cleanliness.
programming school transport;
supervision of school meals supervisory assistants;
detention records and supervision;
dinner places.

[1] Hoyle and McCormick quote Lipham as distinguishing between leaders and administrators on the lines that leaders initiate new structures or procedures to achieve an organizational goal or objective whereas administrators utilize existing structures or procedures for this purpose: Hoyle, Eric and McCormick, Robert, 'Innovation, the School and the Teacher (II)', Units 29-30 of *Curriculum Design and Development*, E203, Open University, 1976, p. 27; Lipham, J., 'Leadership and Administration' in Griffiths, D. (ed.), *Behavioural Science and Educational Administration*, 64th Year Book of the National Society for the Study of Education, Chicago University Press, 1964, p. 122.

Whereas the routine administrative tasks of other levels of responsibility possess a cohesion which comes from their clear relevance to learning objectives, deputy heads are often denied any similar sense of unity of purpose.

Furthermore it is a valid point that a school structure of responsibility is part of the 'hidden curriculum' from which pupils learn. A structure consisting entirely of men (the more likely of the two alternatives because of the greater supply of men career teachers) imparts the message that men are more capable of top educational management than women. It is therefore more consistent with comprehensive school principles of equality and non-discrimination to demonstrate the professional management capacity of both sexes.

Our thinking, however, even in education, remains heavily influenced by assumptions about the innateness or relative permanence of personal characteristics. Whether they be determined genetically or by early environmental influence, the observed personal characteristics of men and women tend to be generalized about and regarded as fixed. The extent to which such characteristics are differently distributed between men and women by the advertisement of commercial products, particularly on television, has frequently been commented on and condemned, not only by representatives of feminist movements. It is true that more women than men are closely involved with the care of children, with nursing, cooking, home-making, cleaning, cosmetics and fashion. Women whose preferences (whether innate or conditioned) lead them to engage in such pursuits may freely do so. That is by no means the same thing as defining a teaching appointment in such a way that women are obliged to conform with this stereotype, or that men are excluded from any participation in matters which are labelled 'feminine preserves'.

Many women deputy heads have in the past found themselves excluded from educational management which their experience has fitted them for and confined to tasks involving the supervision of girls, the care of sick and injured children and the supervision of arrangements for hospitality. If a head identifies the curricular sub-system with learning, the man deputy is frequently put in charge of that structure. A pastoral system which is regarded as furnishing care, welfare and social activities rather than learning often becomes the responsibility of a woman deputy. Some of the damaging consequences of so regarding the school's sub-systems are

considered in Chapter 6. In the present argument, it is enough
to draw attention to the limiting effect such role definitions
have upon the role-holders.

Elizabeth Richardson comments:

This division of strengths, with its implied distribution of weaknesses, was also a reflection of ancient assumptions about mascu-
linity and femininity; for unlike the headships of the lower, middle
and upper schools, these posts were sex-linked. The reason for this
has to be laid at the door, not of the headmaster, but of the Burnham
Committee, which in successive reports has stipulated that if, in a
mixed school, the deputy head is a man, one woman on the staff
may carry the title and responsibility of 'senior mistress' and,
conversely, that if the deputy head is a woman, then one man
on the staff may carry the title and responsibility of 'senior master'.
The unconscious assumption underlying this stipulation appears
to be that a head, whether man or women, must ensure that the
masculine and feminine aspects of his or her leadership are symbo-
lized by the two most senior members of staff. It seems to follow
from this that a headmaster is not allowed his own feminine side
or a headmistress her own masculine side, although all human
beings are to some extent bi-sexual. Thus what looks like a saving
clause to protect a mixed school (and a mixed staff group) from
investing all its top leadership either in two men or in two women,
becomes a trap for the head's Number Two and for the head's
Number Three, binding them in stereotyped roles from which they
find it increasingly more difficult to escape.[1]

In furtherance of the spirit of the 1975 Sex Discrimination
Act, these provisions were omitted from the next Burnham
Report (1977) and no stipulations regarding sex were included. While, therefore, the legal obligation to appoint both men
and women to the top management team of a mixed school
in group 7 or higher was discontinued, the purpose of the
earlier regulation remains unchanged and many appointing
authorities feel a moral imperative to try to fulfil that purpose.

Elizabeth Richardson's comment therefore remains valid
despite the change in the Burnham Report. It matters little
whether a woman (or man) deputy head is appointed as a
legal obligation or as a voluntary demonstration of non-discrimination; the danger of binding that person into a sex-
based stereotype remains a trap.

Schools are institutions which by definition are dedicated
(or should be) to the concept of personal growth; and limiting
roles which cramp senior men and women teachers are
injurious to them, contrary to the objectives which concern
pupils, and inappropriate examples. In the days of expansion
in the 1960s, deputies often accepted uncomplainingly

[1] *The Teacher, The School and the Task of Management*, pp. 218-19.

limiting roles as personal assistants, often with a sexist bias, as a temporary stepping stone to a headship. No doubt they found their experience as deputies of little help to them as preparation for promotion. Now it is more probable that deputies may spend many years at that level of management and may end their teaching careers in that role. A more rational kind of delegation, which was always desirable before, now becomes imperative.

Effective delegation and job satisfaction are closely related. Managers who complain that 'nowadays it is impossible to find responsible subordinates who can be confidently trusted to get on with the job' are usually guilty of failing to create a job from which the holder can hope to gain any satisfaction. An assortment of unrelated chores, the value of which is questioned by others, is often dealt with perfunctorily. The manager then attributes the lack-lustre performance to the personality of the subordinate and further restricts the extent of the responsibility and independence with which he or she was originally entrusted.

Effective delegation demands three qualities: 1. coherence; 2. creativity; and 3. credibility.

1. Coherence

The long list of implementational tasks which fearful heads delegate to deputies clearly demonstrates the meaning of 'incoherence'. The opposite kind of delegation, described as 'coherent', defines an area of responsibility rather than specific tasks which flow from it. The tasks will consequently be related to the same overall purpose. The first practical advantage of coherence is that these tasks, having been devised by the same mind, will mutually support each other, and are less likely to contradict one another than when they are inherited from past practice and may have been originally initiated by more than one person. The second advantage of coherence is that it is easier for all other members of an institution to attach to a particular deputy an area of responsibility rather than a list of diverse tasks. The school which delegates tasks, especially unrelated collections of tasks, needs to issue to its staff a detailed directory of who does what. Much valuable time can be wasted consulting this sort of directory when a teacher wants to enlist the assistance of a deputy.

Coherence may be achieved by starting from a consideration of the aims and objectives of the school. Between

them, the members of a top management team should aim
to be responsible for the whole management of the school.
The top management may consist of the head and five or
six other members (three deputies and two or three senior
teachers). Their approach may be to consider the broad
needs of the school and to negotiate together which of these
needs each member other than the head feels most fitted
to meet. (The role of the head of a school is considered
later in this chapter.) Such divisions of responsibility must
depend as much if not more upon the number of teachers
involved and upon their skills than upon any abstract ideal
of a pre-existing pattern. The division will therefore have a
degree of arbitrariness about it. The responsibilities may
be grouped and packaged in many different ways. Possible
roles might include:

1. curriculum development;
2. resources (time-table, staffing, materials, library etc.);
3. community relations (PTA, careers, liaison with other
   schools and external agencies, colleges, universities,
   youth clubs, the media etc.);
4. professional tutor (in charge of staff development, teacher appraisal, student teachers, probationary teachers,
   in-service training);
5. evaluation, assessment and examinations.

Since the management of a school is itself an essentially
indivisible coherent whole which concerns the learning of
all the individuals in it, all responsibilities are interdependent
and overlap. To that extent, divisions are artificial. The top
management must work as a coherent body, knowing each
other's work and framing their actions to be consistent with
those of all other members.

At this top management level, as in the work of the
departments and pastoral units, delegation, if it devolves
significant responsibility, is the most important form of
in-service training. Unlike short courses away from the
school (useful though these often are) delegation is training
which is 'in-service' in every sense of the term.

When members of a top management group work closely
together with roles that are coherent, they are effectively
learning the responsibility of headship. Although narrow
competence in a deputy's own personal role should not
result when continuous consultation is engaged in, it may

be desirable that roles be exchanged every two or three years to broaden experience. The promotion of any member of the group to a post outside the school provides an opportunity for a reconsideration of the roles and their allocation to the individual members.

The important difference between well-conceived delegated roles and soul-destroying ones is not that the former contain no implementational tasks (normally called 'administration') but that in the former such tasks are a means to an end rather than being an end in themselves. The process which has been described derives particular roles from general aims or from a general survey of aspects of the school's responsibility. It may therefore be called a deductive method. This method is appropriate when the generalized responsibilities of a school have already been reliably surveyed. This is comparatively rare in our highly decentralized system of education where only vague, often conflicting assumptions exist about what schools are for, and it is left to practising teachers to define their own primary task.

It is likely that most top management groups will find it easier to adopt an inductive method, deriving the more general from the particular. Schools have in the past been run empirically. Tasks have been recognized, often randomly undertaken by heads and deputies, and in the pressing urgency of keeping the enterprise working, there has been little time to philosophize about general principles. In such circumstances a top management group may choose to take the actual tasks performed as their starting point rather than a broad conceptualization of the purpose of the school derived from a set of aims and objectives. If this method is adopted, each individual task might be written on a separate piece of paper. Then jobs which appear related to each other might be gathered together. This is a sophisticated game of 'happy families' played by head, deputies and senior teachers in which the 'family' does not obtain a name until there has been an analysis of what each family member has in common with the others. When the 'members' of a family (the individual tasks) and the 'family name' (the area of responsibility) have both been finally settled, together they constitute a job description which should be recorded and circulated to all staff members. This enables the whole staff to identify which member of the top management team to go to for help, advice and action without having to memorize or refer to a long list of individual duties.

2. Creativity

Tasks are sometimes sub-divided into those concerning the maintenance of a system and those which create and develop a system. There is always a greater sense of achievement in the latter kind of activity as this contains the creative element. Every delegated role must involve a quota of maintenance tasks but should also offer the opportunity to make an imaginative contribution to the fulfilment of the school's aims. The contribution may not be direct but, in the case of senior posts, may often be the creation of a programme or procedure designed to make the work of others more effective and sometimes designed to make it easier. When the top management team can feel that, by means of consultation about the problems experienced by colleagues, they can help to resolve them by the use of insight and imagination, they also experience personal satisfaction. This experience is denied to people in routine jobs whose every action is prescribed from above. It should not be the monopoly, as it often is, of classroom teachers, heads of departments and heads, and be outside the experience of deputy heads.

Members of top management teams are often allocated a lighter than average teaching time-table to enable them to discharge wider responsibilities. This lightened time-table renders them vulnerable to criticism that they are either idle during their 'free periods' or are engaged in unnecessary 'administrative' tasks. All leadership roles are subject to mixed feelings from the group members. Members feel torn between the desire to co-operate with leaders who are able and willing to help them and resentment at being dependent upon them for such help. It is therefore essential that heads of schools should bear this in mind when discussing the nature of the roles to be fulfilled by members of the top management team. Deputies who are denied the opportunity to create ways of helping their colleagues are exposed to all the resentment and receive none of the co-operation.

3. Credibility

Three developments over recent years have led to the creation of a certain number of ill-defined 'non-jobs'. One is the expansion of above-basic scale posts following the enlargement of a number of comparatively small schools or the merging of two or more schools into one. This has often been accompanied by the need to absorb relatively highly paid grammar and secondary-modern school deputy heads, senior masters or mistresses and heads of department into a new pattern of responsibilities considered appropriate for a comprehensive school. The second phenomenon has been the explosion of new needs, or apparent needs, accompanying comprehensive reorganization, the widening of objectives and the increasing complexity of staff structures. The third is the belief which has gained a certain currency that long service and competent classroom teaching ought to be rewarded by salary scales above scale 1 without the acceptance of any special responsibility.

The first development concerning staff transferred from the bipartite to a comprehensive system has sometimes given rise to a secondary-modern school senior mistress or deputy head being nominated as a 'deputy head–pastoral' in the comprehensive organization. There are instances of men being given pastoral roles of this kind, but women deputy heads seem to have been especially vulnerable. Following such an appointment a whole network of heads of upper, middle and lower school, year heads or housemasters and mistresses is also created, so depriving the pastoral head of any effective role, leaving her stranded high and dry without an effective function.

The second development, that is, the growing complexity of staff structures in comprehensive schools to meet an awareness of new needs, often led to a feeling of isolation and fragmentation. In such circumstances teachers can feel a danger of being out of touch with what others are doing, or even possibly of being undermined by the others, whose efforts may be thought to be pulling in the opposite direction from their own. It seems likely that this is the explanation for the large number of vacancies for 'co-ordinators' of various kinds advertised during recent years in the press. It would be wrong to imply that all such posts are ill-defined 'non-jobs'; but it is virtually certain that, in many cases, the relationship of the co-ordinator with those whose work he or she is supposed to be co-ordinating often suffers from inadequate definition. Besides posts created to try to meet feelings of isolation, there are probably many others invented in a desperate search for ways of meeting other needs, or even simply in response to fashion or the desire to compete with other schools in the district. To determine whether these are credible posts or non-jobs, the test is how the rest of the teachers in the school regard the role-holder after a year or more experience of his or her activities. If teachers are aware that the post and its holder have assisted the effectiveness of their work, the post is a credible one. If not, it may be tempting to attribute the blame to the personality of the role-holder rather than to the role itself. However, no personality however dynamic can display his or her qualities in a non-job. On the other hand many an unpromising personality has proved effective and has developed out of all recognition when entrusted with a responsibility that is seen by everyone to be needed and worth doing.

There have been examples in most people's experience of the third category of 'non-jobs'. Those who have maintained that increased status and remuneration in the formal system ought to recognize undefined personal qualities rather than specific responsibilities have often urged upon heads that promotion to higher scales should be justified by the invention of some plausible but in reality non-existent role. Heads of department are often tempted to urge this device in their natural anxiety to retain a promising young teacher who has reached the stage of seeking promotion and will move to another school if it is not available in his present one. If the promising young teacher has already obtained promotion by being appointed to another school, and especially if he teaches a shortage subject like mathematics or science, the economics of the market-place may suggest the need to invent a responsibility in order to 'buy in' a rare commodity. A head of department who feels anxiety of this kind (and it is a very natural and often wholly justified anxiety) should bear in mind when advising the head that it will be a positive disservice to the retained promising young teacher (or his replacement if he has already gone) to invent a job which lacks credibility. If he can do nothing effective and professional to assist his colleagues in their work, his promotion is bound to be resented in the long run however popular he or she may be personally. Perhaps it is not at all common nowadays, but there was a time in secondary schools when scale (or 'score') posts were allotted ostensibly for 'taking fifth-year examination work' or for 'sixth-form teaching' (tasks shared widely by other teachers not so rewarded, or rewarded for other real responsibilities). In reality posts of this kind may often have been thinly disguised bait to induce the holder not to move for another year or two. The head of department who seeks promotion for certain of his colleagues should, then, avoid selecting as the reason responsibilities shared by many other teachers. He should also detect and evade the trap of designating menial, often clerical, chores as the sole justification for a delegated role within the department. This trap involves failing to satisfy the criterion of 'professional creativity' which we have seen to be a common fault in the definition of the tasks of deputy heads. Maintenance tasks of this kind might be 'responsibility for the departmental stock cupboard' or 'for copying, maintaining and distributing set lists'.

A credible job at any level, besides being coherent and giving scope for professional decisions, must be perceived by other members of the institution or department to be necessary and helpful to their work. A head of department in the circumstances we have described must be prepared to surrender by delegation some aspect of his work which is coherent, creative and credible. This aspect might concern an age-range of pupils or an aspect of the work of the department. In the first category might be the syllabus and resources of years 1 and 2 together with liaison with the contributory primary schools to ensure continuity. In the second category of delegation, a head of mathematics might surrender his responsibility for work in statistics or computers.

At this point the use of the word 'surrender' suggests the need to consider what conditions are necessary for successful delegation. The interests of the holder of a delegated role imply that the one who delegates should make a real sacrifice of day-to-day control and of frequent intervention with instructions about what to do next. It should be enough that the subordinate has had his responsibilities clearly defined and that he or she is aware of and committed to the overall objectives of the department. It goes without saying that anyone delegating responsibility for an age-range or a sub-aspect of the work of a school, a year group or a department must ensure that the subordinate is granted all the resources of time, materials, space and equipment required by the job with which he or she is entrusted. It is also the responsibility of the one who delegates to define as clearly as possible the extent of autonomous decision-making granted to the subordinate and any requirement that certain other people should be consulted in advance. In addition it is the duty of the one who delegates to inform everyone concerned of the specification of the delegated role. (For instance, in the case of the delegation of departmental work in years 1 and 2, this information must obviously be conveyed to contributory primary schools as well as to all those remotely needing to know in the secondary school itself.)

Delegation raises the problem of accountability. It has been said that the one who delegates a sphere of responsibility must not seek to retain control of that sphere by personal intervention. He nevertheless remains accountable for the conduct of all such delegated fields of activity. This is what makes many leaders reluctant to delegate. Of course the holder of a delegated role is also accountable, in this case to the leader who has done the delegating. There are sometimes complaints from heads of schools that they cannot entrust responsible roles to their colleagues because it is so difficult to find teachers willing and able to take on responsibility. Of course we all feel that we could do almost anything better ourselves, but heads of large schools and heads of large departments have to face the reality that the jobs which they should properly be undertaking will not get done effectively if they attempt to do too much themselves. If delegation seems not to be working any manager has to try to find out why. It is his responsibility to make it work; that is why he remains accountable. He should ask himself:

1. Is the delegated role a proper one characterized by coherence, creativity and credibility?
2. Has the area of responsibility been clearly defined?
3. Is it fully understood by the role-holder and all others concerned?
4. Have I refrained from frequent interference? In other words do I trust the role-holder as a responsible person rather than as a servant?
5. Have I ensured that all the resources required by the

task are available — time, space, materials, people, equipment and perhaps funds?

6. Has the institution provided adequate opportunities for the role-holder to acquire the skills and experience required by the task?

If the answer to all these questions is a truthful 'yes' then the role-holder has probably failed in his stewardship; but the manager who delegated to him may rightly be held accountable too for choosing the wrong person for the task.

Heads

The most common model of articles of government states that

> the headteacher shall be responsible to the governors for the general direction of the conduct and curriculum of the school. Subject to the provisions of these articles and the regulations of the Local Education Authority, the headteacher shall control the internal organisation, management and discipline of the school, shall exercise supervision over the teaching and non-teaching staff other than the post of clerk to the governors and shall have the power of suspending pupils from attendance for any cause which he considers adequate, but on the suspension of any pupil a report of the case shall forthwith be made to the governors, who shall thereupon consult the Local Education Authority.

The articles require there to be full consultation and co-operation at all times between the headteacher, the chairman of the governors and the Chief Education Officer. There is a further requirement that all major proposals and reports affecting the conduct and curriculum of the school should be submitted by the headteacher to the governors and the Chief Education Officer.

It is clear therefore that a head is accountable for every aspect of the life of the school and for consulting with the governors and the LEA on every important issue. This brief is so wide and yet apparently so precise that heads have often felt it unnecessary to define for their colleagues the details of their own role. Yet, in large schools where so much is delegated to deputy heads, senior teachers, heads of faculties, departments, house or year heads, the suspicion may grow that the head of the school finished his task when he wound up the clock and set it going. If he fails to define what he has *not* delegated he may be regarded as a kind of deity who has created a world in six days and then enjoys an eternal sabbath during which he surveys it and finds that it is good. Indeed many heads may delegate only half-heartedly, or take back what has been given away for fear of creating an unendurable vacuum in their own lives. In reality institutions composed of human beings, especially adolescent ones, rarely run on as predicted in the design drawing. Consequently problems requiring the head's decisions constantly present themselves. There may nevertheless be a real fear that comprehensive delegation may result in a vacuum relieved only by a succession of unforeseen crises.

Heads need to consider what they will reserve for their personal attention and what they will not delegate. Though they may decide not to delegate certain areas this does not, of course, mean that they are precluded from consulting others before taking action. Indeed consultation of colleagues may be implicit in their view of the role of head teacher.

Like every other role-holder, heads, too, need coherence, creativity and credibility. The central coherence and creativity of the head's role stem from the fact that the institution for which he or she is responsible is essentially and pre-eminently an *educational* one. That is to say it is dedicated to the growth and development of all its members, teachers, pupils and non-teaching staff alike. The primary co-ordinating principle, therefore, which will assist a head to define a role for himself, is the acknowledgement that the role is that of an *educator*. This view is likely to be more helpful than the idea, for instance, that he or she is primarily a meticulous administrator. Besides discouraging good teachers who have found teaching a satisfying occupation from seeking headship, the view of a head as an administrator presents only half the truth. While administrative skills are valuable in heads, they are only productive if harnessed to the fulfilment of a worthwhile purpose. They are no more and no less worthy of emphasis in the head's role than in that of the teacher or the head of department. The purpose of all teaching roles is the learning of the members of the group. There are frequently authoritarian expectations imposed upon heads, not only by the public and the media but also by some members of the teaching profession. This view of heads as ordering, controlling, instructing and disciplining from a position of superior knowledge and power is a natural extension of the traditional view of the teacher's role in relation to pupils. So far, it is unfortunate that the gradual evolution of the concept of the teacher's role from that of the transmitter of knowledge to that of the facilitator of learning has not yet brought about a similar change in the understanding of the role of the head.

There are, of course, problems about conceiving of the head's role as primarily that of an educator of teachers. A teacher can legitimately expect that his knowledge of his subject, of children's stages of development and of how children learn should be recognized as superior to the knowledge possessed by pupils. It is not as easy to identify the subject in which a head may claim superior knowledge. However even in the teacher's role, the possession of factual knowledge is regarded in these times of the 'explosion of knowledge' as less important than the awareness of where the knowledge required is to be found and the skills to guide the pupil into how to obtain access to this knowledge. This awareness and these skills can be said to be of prime importance in a head's task of promoting the learning of his or her colleagues on the teaching staff. In the same way the teacher's understanding of the stages of pupil development and of how they learn most effectively needs to be paralleled by the head's understanding of the stages of teachers' development and of how they learn most effectively.

A further problem which arises in conceiving of the head's role as primarily that of educator in relation to teachers as well as in relation to pupils resides in the still common assumption that the making of a teacher is a task external to the school, confined to universities, colleges and polytechnics. Following the James Report has come the recognition that initial training is only the first stage in a life-long process. In-service training, INSET, school-focused, school-based training and the broader concept of staff development are now increasingly recognized as school responsibilities, and should be stated explicitly in the aims and objectives of the school. If the role of the 'manager' (in the technical language of management) is 'the maximization of resources for the fulfilment of specified objectives' then it must be recognized that the school's most valuable resources are its teachers. The head's role in ensuring staff development may be said to be 'maximizing' these resources.

In order to ensure staff development the head's first task must be to consult his colleagues and stimulate their thinking

about aims and objectives. Selznik in *Leadership in Administration* (1957) describes a leader as being

> responsible for defining the mission of the enterprise, for building
> the special values of the enterprise which reinforce the drives towards
> fulfilling the mission, and for developing a distinctive competence
> of the enterprise to carry out its mission.[1]

A. K. Rice in *The Enterprise and its Environment* adds

> The institutional leader is primarily an expert in the promotion
> and protection of values and has the major task of reconciling
> the internal strivings of the members of the institution and the
> pressures that are exerted on them by the external environment.[2]

In order to do this it will be necessary as a second task to
set up clearly understood consultative machinery. While
much valuable consultation can be achieved by informal
methods, it remains essential to devise formal methods
too. More will be said about this in Chapter 7. The aim in
establishing such machinery and in establishing aims and
objectives is to stimulate as widespread as possible a common
sense of purpose and commitment to this purpose. Teachers
who have contributed to a careful appraisal of their shared
task and are encouraged by the head's view of his or her
own role as an educator to discuss this task and modify it from
time to time in the light of changed needs are likely to
grow in professional stature and in their sense of
responsibility.

Thirdly, a head will normally wish to be closely involved
in the selection of all members of the teaching staff. The
criteria which will mainly influence the 'educator-head' will
be the evidence, some impressionistic and some objective, of
experience and skills and personal qualities which seem likely
to grow in the conditions provided by the school concerned.
Heads are not normally autonomous in the appointment of
teaching staff. For senior appointments, the Local Education
Authority and the governors have an important part to play.
In more junior appointments heads who consider the role
as an extension of that of the teacher will wish to involve
middle-management department and pastoral heads in

---

[1] Selznik, P., *Leadership in Administration*, Row, Peterson, Evanston, Illinois,
1957.
[2] Rice, A. K., *The Enterprise and its Environment*, Tavistock Publications,
1963, p. 203.

specifying the needs of the vacancy, describing it in an advertisement or in an explanation sent with the application forms in answer to enquiries, in scrutinizing applications, in short-listing and in interviewing.

Fourthly, a head whose main concern is the promotion of the skills and effectiveness of his colleagues will consult them with a view to devising a structure of staff responsibilities which recognize and attempt to fulfil the aims and objectives of the school by utilizing the past experience of staff and extending their latent potential skills.

Fifthly, the head will accept responsibility for all policy decisions made by anyone in the school with the intention of furthering its aims and objectives. Decisions which concern the whole institution he or she will regard as a personal responsibility. (A later chapter on 'consultation' discusses the conditions which necessarily accompany such decisions.) Many other teachers, both senior and junior, and pupils themselves, are constantly making decisions within the intended framework of delegation. Their authority to do so stemming 'from above' is the delegation authorized by the head, and 'from below' their authority is based upon the extent to which their decisions are perceived as helpful to the aspirations of those who are subject to the decisions. Previous discussion about accountability suggests that the head's role in determining the staff structure of delegation concerning a wide range of decisions also involves him or her in the responsibility of continuous support, arbitration, negotiation and perhaps occasionally modification of this structure in areas where the nature of the decisions being made is frequently called in question by the members in whose interest they ought to be made.

The sixth main responsibility of the head is to keep in close touch with the world outside the school from which the pupils (and the teachers) come and to which they go temporarily at the end of each day, for longer periods at the end of each term, and permanently when they leave. The principal representatives of this outside world are the members of the governing body and the officers of the local education authority. In addition there are other important individuals and bodies such as HM Inspectorate, the Parent/ Teacher Association, local employers, examination boards, and many others. The head will consider himself personally responsible for consulting with governors and the LEA about the aims and objectives of the school and about methods of appraising the extent to which these are being achieved. To people who hold traditional assumptions about the nature of 'teaching', particularly the superior/inferior relationships thought to be inseparable from it, the head's responsibility towards governors may seem fundamentally different from the task of a teacher. The head will obtain, classify and present to the governing body information relevant to the purpose in hand, highlight problems and point to methods of arriving at individual, autonomous, rational judgements. It is suggested that virtually the same description could be used of the methods of a teacher of history, social studies, literature, science and most school subjects. Whether or not one can accept that a head 'teaches' his governors depends upon one's definition of teaching.

Heads of schools are prone to the use of metaphors when referring to their job. They frequently see themselves as 'captains of the ship' (preferably a happy ship) but also as desk-bound bureaucrats burdened with returns and forms to fill. The public and the media tend to see them as a combination of judge and jury and chief prison warder, if not executioner (in cases of pupil indiscipline). Many heads yearn nostalgically for the carefree days when they were protected by the four walls of a classroom from telephones, forms, inspectors, advisers, parents and teachers with grievances. When they claim to be *primus inter pares* in relationship to the teaching staff, it is sometimes without conviction, for they feel obliged to admit that the token teaching timetable which they cling to like a port in a storm hardly entitles them to be regarded as teachers still. No wonder headship is seen as threatened by a cloud of disillusionment! How natural that promotion from deputy headship to headship should seem to decree the final abandonment as no longer appropriate of all the teaching skills acquired by a lifetime of diligent practice (up to that point)! How absurd that governors should consider successful teaching experience as a criterion in selecting applicants for headship! How much more sensible it would be to seek candidates for headship from among the ranks of competent civil servants, retired army officers or successful managers in commerce and industry!

This concept of the headship role has led to widespread if suppressed uneasiness in the teaching profession and has undermined confidence in our own rationality. Most teachers would fight hard to retain the post of leadership of a school community as the summit of the teaching career within the school system. Yet many have doubts about the existence of any correlation between a teacher's experience and the functions of a head. Many suspect that the title 'head teacher' is a concessionary misnomer.

The same uneasiness in a somewhat blunted form besets teachers on their promotion to any management role as a head of faculty, department, house or year or deputy head. The 'pupil-teaching' part of the role is still significant enough for them for the dilemma to appear, in more muted tones. It remains true that their management tasks in relation to the other teachers in the department or pastoral unit tend to be regarded as remote from teaching.

To summarize this analysis, it may be said that, in schools, teaching is management and management is teaching. To effect this equation all that is necessary is to discard four elements in the traditional view of teaching which are, in any case, largely superseded in our more lucid views about it. Firstly, teaching is not necessarily didactic or instructional. Secondly, teaching is not exclusively mediated to inferiors by superiors. Thirdly teaching is not solely an activity conducted by adults for the benefit of children. Fourthly, teaching is not confined to classrooms, laboratories, studios, workshops, gymnasia and playing fields. It is any activity in which one person uses skills, knowledge and appropriate methods and resources to provide opportunities for others to gain mastery and understanding in a chosen sphere of facts, concepts, attitudes and skills — and it can take place anywhere!

All management of teaching involves delegation of various kinds, as we have already discussed. The most obvious example of this is the complex curricular and pastoral systems which have been created in schools. In the next chapter we shall consider some problems which arise from prevalent misconceptions of the purposes of such systems and their relationship with each other.

6 Pastoral and Curricular Sub-Systems

Heads of schools have always delegated responsibilities to teachers. In the very small school a class teacher may have delegated to him responsiblity for co-ordinating the growth and development of the children in his class. Even in the small school which has specialist teachers but no departments different teachers are entrusted with certain subject areas in relation to the classes which they teach and are also given a 'form' to look after. Their job was (and still is in the very small school) to register the children's attendance daily, supervise their punctuality and their appearance and check that they are suitably equipped and ready for the day's task of learning. In addition the form teacher reads and summarizes progress reports prepared by subject teachers, and communicates with parents. What has been described is a 'single-order system' with a 'first stage of differentiation'. Each class or form is an 'operating system'. The terms used are those of A. K. Rice in *The Enterprise and its Environment*.[1]

In a single-order system like the small school, therefore, the head, deputy head and all class and subject teachers form the overall management. The class and subject teachers' functions are performed by the same people assuming different roles in relation to forms or classes of pupils according to the demands of the time-table and the routine of the school day. A one-form entry school catering for a seven-year age-range would thus have seven classes. The management group with head and deputy would consist of nine people, perhaps ten to allow for marking and preparation periods. A two-form entry school would have a management group of eighteen or nineteen. The most significant feature of the single-order school is that the top management (head and deputy) relates directly to the basic level of management

[1] Tavistock Publications, 1963.

without intermediaries. There are no discrete 'operating systems' other than the forms and classes themselves. In such a system the top management does not delegate any tasks of co-ordination in respect of the responsibilities of the basic level, but undertakes it itself. Such a system presupposes that top management has competence to manage the two elements in the school's task: (1) technical expertise in the content and methods of the curriculum, and (2) personal knowledge of the progress and needs of each pupil. It is doubtful whether top management in the secondary school ever did possess the technical expertise required to manage the content and methods of all aspects of the curriculum. In most grammar schools, *de facto* management of this (before the institution of subject departments) was operated by the public examination boards. Heads and deputies put most of their time and energies into knowing pupils individually and supervising their progress.

The development of a sub-system based upon subject departments probably arose from two main causes. Firstly, the expertise required to manage all the different aspects of the curriculum made increasing demands upon the time of heads and deputies and upon their training, which was rarely sufficiently broad to ensure their competence. Secondly the advent of secondary-modern schools, where, at least at first, no public examinations were taken, revealed the need for curricular management to fulfil the role performed by the examinations in the grammar schools. When heads of department were appointed there came into being one kind of sub-system based upon subject skills; this is the second order of differentiation.

The establishment of the departmental first-order operating and managing system in effect interposes an order between the time-tabled class (studying a subject) and the top management. The class, formerly a first-order differentiation, then became a second-order differentiation. The other operating system — the form managed by its form master or mistress — remained for many years as a first-order differentiation with no intervening order which would have made it into a second-order differentiation.

It was the creation of much larger schools in the maintained system which emphasized the inability of top management to manage directly any longer the other operating system, which required the supervision of the progress of pupils in all their learning. Had these children all been selected on the assumption of a similar level of ability and hence of similar educational needs, the problem would not have appeared quite as acute. The top management of comprehensive schools realized that their pupils came from widely different backgrounds, had reached very different levels of attainment on admission, and that the social and environmental conditions affecting their ability to learn varied from the entirely favourable to the destructively disadvantageous. The management of the learning of such pupils demanded a more intimate knowledge of their stages of development and more sensitive handling of the experiences the school hoped to afford them. That, together with the greatly increased numbers, inevitably brought about the 'further differentiation' into a second-order system of the form master/mistress management task.

This management system is not related, like the curricular one, to skills and experience in subject areas. Instead it is based upon sub-groupings of pupils within the whole institution. Faced with the new problem of how to sub-divide the pupils in the whole school, heads of schools looked around for precedents. In the public boarding schools there was considerable experience of sub-systems based upon pupil groupings.

The need in the public boarding schools for such a sub-system had arisen partly from size (many of the most famous schools contained more than 1,000 boys), partly from the practical problems of providing manageable units of accommodation, and partly from the competitive philosophy upon which such schools are often based. This type of management sub-system entrusted to housemasters responsibility for a 'vertical' cross-section of boys representing the full age-range for which the school catered. The admission of new pupils to one house rather than another could be said to be arbitrary in that clear criteria for allocation were rarely stated — though family traditions, where these existed, were taken into account. Also there was normally a desire to try to ensure an equal sharing-out of potential athletic and academic talent so that competition could take place between the sub-units on equal terms.

This method of sub-dividing the school into management units was widely adopted in the early days of comprehensive re-organization by the maintained schools concerned. It is normally called the 'house system' by analogy with the residential accommodation of the public schools (often converted from former family residences in the less affluent boarding schools). It is interesting to conjecture about the possible reasons for the popularity of the choice of house systems in comprehensive schools rather than the age-differentiated 'year system', examples of which were also readily available in the maintained system in different forms in the separate infant, junior, and middle schools. Some observers of the secondary scene in the 1950s and 1960s would point to the numbers of heads of schools, particularly of grammar schools, and local-authority administrators, who were the products of the public-school system. They would conclude that such people were drawing upon their own experience as pupils in the choice they made. In this decision, as in so many others, the prestige attaching to the public schools in the eyes of society was a strong factor, no doubt, in influencing heads to imitate them. Indeed maintained day schools, both grammar and secondary-modern, had felt the need for competitive sub-units for a very long time. Most secondary schools already had 'house systems' which were the basis of games and athletics. In some cases such competitive activities extended to drama, music, verse-speaking, charitable fund-raising and even examination results, merit marks, and attendance and punctuality. As such schools became comprehensive the competitive philosophy was often transferred from the old situation to the new one. Belief in such a philosophy was reinforced by the general assumption (endorsed by the House of Commons resolution of 21 January 1965 quoted in DES Circular 10/65) that comprehensive education was to preserve all that was valuable in grammar-school education. On the whole such forms of *team* competition as have been mentioned probably had few harmful effects upon the self-esteem and motivation of the losers even when they lost (as some did) consistently for considerable periods. That such destructive effects *are* possible, however, is indicated by the extreme case of the supporters of Scottish Association football in the World Cup series in Argentina in 1978 when the disintegration of morale was accompanied by a search for scapegoats as irrational as a witch hunt. The recovery of co-operative purpose displayed in the last game against Holland reflected an outstanding sense of inward confidence in themselves in the players and little credit upon their 'supporters'. At this point it is simply

worth noting that the original reason for 'houses' (the need
for manageable units of accommodation), together with the
justification for calling them 'houses' at all, had long been
either forgotten or overlaid by a set of new assumptions and
expectations which had little to do with the origins of this
type of management system.

Though team competition based upon houses may in
most cases have had few, if any, damaging effects and certainly continues to have positive value in sports activities,
other consequences of the House as a management system
can be seen in retrospect to have been a potential source of
conflict and confusion in the formulation and practice
of aims, in the task of management and the consultative
machinery set up.

When competition on a team basis is closely associated
with a management system, it has a tendency to be diffused
into individual rivalries, and personal competition may be
similarly institutionalized. In comprehensive schools where
the dice are not impartial and chances are unequally distributed, the effect is likely, on balance, to undermine the voluntary involvement of many pupils. What may be acceptable
and even usefully stimulating to adults, who have already
established a sense of identity to which they assent, may
often provoke the end of effort and active co-operation
among adolescents. Advocates of the competitive house
system have not always been aware of the need to define
with care the limits of competition. In general terms, its
usefulness is confined to situations in which chances are
really equal and to activities in which the self-esteem of
individual pupils is not too deeply committed.

The task of management may also be unnecessarily compli-
cated and even frustrated by misconceptions which have
frequently accompanied vertical house systems. Again,
deriving from the public school with its peculiar boarding
needs and from a network of semantic confusions, the
management system by houses came increasingly to be
regarded as the repository of the caring role of the teacher
in his responsibility to act *in loco parentis*. The quasi-paternal
relationship of a housemaster (and the quasi-maternal one of
his wife) with the boys in his house fulfils an important
need arising from the absence of natural parents in a boarding
school. For the fairly long stretches of time, afternoons
before prep and week-ends after midday, when the boys

are not in classes, the housemaster and his wife provide a substitute family and the house (with all the warm, comforting associations of the word if not always of the dormitory accommodation itself) provides the friendships, the activities and the refuge which day boys receive from their homes.

These overtones of comfort, protection and love became so woven into the concept of the house management subsystem in comprehensive day schools, that the phrase 'pastoral care' was coined to identify its assumed function. The phrase, as so often happens, rapidly came to be accepted as embodying a self-evident truth, and in its turn reinforced the comforting attitudes of those holding responsibility in the structure. 'Pastoral' in its educational context has inherited a vast tradition of associations pertaining to agriculture and religion and literature. The Good Shepherd who looks after his flock, neglecting the ninety-and-nine in the fold to seek the one who is lost, who makes his sheep lie down in green pastures and leads them beside the still waters, the pastor who has spiritual care of his 'flock', the simplicity and natural charm of sunlit meadows and the 'sound of pastoral reed with oaten stops' have all woven their threads into the expectations which others have of those engaged in 'pastoral care'. No doubt those so engaged have had similar conscious or unconscious assumptions about themselves, as well as responding to the expectations of others. When a physics teacher can give up his post as a head of department to become a housemaster on the grounds that he 'loves children', it is clear that he feels the house post will afford greater scope for his sympathetic concern than his departmental post. The phrase 'pastoral care' has become so deeply embedded in educational jargon that it is equally often used to describe a 'horizontal' year system, and has survived its detachment from the original association with public-school residential houses.

It is not intended to argue that a deepening consciousness in teachers of their responsibility to adopt desirable parental attitudes of protection, sympathy and tolerance is a bad thing — only that the effect of making this caring quality synonymous with pastoral systems is to deny that it is equally a part of the role of all teachers fulfilling teaching functions in the curriculum management sub-system. When engaged in rational discussion, teachers frequently point to evidence of this caring attitude at work in the classroom and deny that the practical effects of identifying house or year systems with caring are in any way detrimental. Fortunately this may well be true. The danger is not that teachers in classrooms will become inhuman machines but that attitudes of caring, challenging, encouraging, criticizing, understanding, demanding, assessing and consoling — inextricably interwoven in all good teaching practice, whatever may be the role relationship of the moment — should be separated out in people's minds as characteristic of discrete management units. In crude terms, there may be a danger that classroom teachers will feel that in perceiving their pupils as living, individual people they are encroaching upon the domain of the pastoral system. Such is the resilience of human nature that they will probably do nothing to change their practice, but they may be subject to insidious, subconscious resentments that there exists a system which, in the eyes at least of some, only justifies itself at the cost of depriving them of some of the most rewarding aspects of their work.

There are other instances in the practice of school management which indicate that essential aspects of the role of all teachers, whatever function they may be fulfilling at a given time, are inhibited whenever such aspects are specifically allotted to a discrete sub-system. Some examples are worth mentioning of which teachers are more aware than of the disadvantages of entrusting their caring attitudes to the pastoral system. The first example is that of counselling. Following the establishment of courses in counselling by a number of universities and colleges, there is evidence of uncertainty about whether the teachers trained in such courses should use the insights and skills acquired in their normal roles or whether their skills would be wasted if they were not employed as full-time counsellors. Much of the opposition to the appointment of full-time counsellors is based upon the belief that the designation of such a specified function may deter other teachers from using their counselling skills. One's standpoint on this question is likely to be determined by the extent to which one believes that a course of training (often one year full-time) has fostered significantly greater skills, and the confidence one has that a specialist counsellor can share his or her skills with colleagues without claiming a monopoly of counselling relationships with pupils.

Similarly the existence of a discrete management sub-unit, usually called 'the English Department', with a designated responsibility for the development of language skills, has, in practice if not in theory, diminished the attention paid by teachers in other departments to this important aspect of learning. In recommending a whole school policy of 'language across the curriculum', the Bullock Report[1] had the difficult task of promoting the recognition of the responsibility of all teachers for language development without depriving the English Department of its primary task, and with it its very *raison d'être*.

'Caring' as the primary task of the pastoral system poses a similar dilemma between the alternatives of making the curriculum system uncaring or leaving pastoral care without a *raison d'être*.

It is arguable that the original reason for identifying pastoral systems with caring embodies the same principle of a discrete management sub-system being attributed with exclusive rights over the operation which it is assumed to perform. The operation of pupil learning is, of course, vested in the whole school. The departmental or curricular sub-system could be perceived, as long as it was the only sub-system, as fulfilling subordinate tasks within the general purpose of pupil learning. With the establishment of a second kind of sub-system (conceived in terms of sub-groups of pupils) it was concluded that its task could *not* be pupil learning since that was already bespoken. Encroachment by one sub-system upon the domain of another is always regarded as a threat to be resisted. The task of caring was accordingly separated off from learning and the divorce was ratified by the title 'Pastoral' for the new system.

Elizabeth Richardson illustrates the process.

The evolution of the pastoral system as many teachers know it, seems to have been accompanied by a notion that the tutorial or 'caring' function should be as free as possible from work associations. The strange institution of 'moral tutors' in certain universities rests on this same belief: that the pupil (young or old) can be 'known' as a person and therefore helped as a person more effectively if the caring adult does not also have to teach him mathematics

[1] DES, *A Language for Life*, HMSO, 1975.

or science or French or English or any other subject. This seems
to be a questionable assumption.[1]

There is evidence in the things teachers say on in-service
training courses that pastoral middle managers are regarded
with some resentment by heads of curricular departments
and by junior teachers. Holders of both these roles accept
their other responsibilities as form tutors in the pastoral
system. They nevertheless often see little need for any
form of management of these functions. It would seem
that so far we have failed to provide an adequate specification of the job of pastoral middle managers. Although
few teachers would deny that pastoral year and house heads
are busy enough, they are sometimes perceived as performing routine clerical functions which could as easily be fulfilled by ancillary staff. Because year and house heads have
rarely been offered or derived for themselves a clear pattern
of aims (other than an imprecise aura of goodwill towards
pupils and a set of routine maintenance tasks) they may
have found it difficult at the next stage to define the aims
of form tutors in precise terms. As a consequence they
have been handicapped in their role of facilitating the form-
tutor role. When the leadership and authority of year and
house heads is only grudgingly acknowledged or is denied,
the reason may not lie in the personalities of the pastoral
heads themselves but in uncertainties about the purposes
of the pastoral system. Such uncertainties might be expected
to result in a lack of common purpose shared by members
of a pastoral team and hence in an absence of any recognition of a need for leadership in achieving it. The authority
of a pastoral head may be said to derive from his effectiveness in enabling form tutors to be effective form tutors.

We appear to be in need of a more precise awareness of
what purpose is served or should be served by the management sub-system which we call 'pastoral care'. An attempt
has been made to show its development from a two-tier
management system into a three-tier one. Its origins lie in
the need for a management system defined in terms of
pupils rather than curricular subject areas.

In an analysis of the structure of complex systems, Miller

[1] Richardson, E., *The Teacher, the School and the Task of Management*,
Heinemann, 1973, p. 108.

(1959), as quoted by A. K. Rice in *The Enterprise and its Environment* (1963), detects three possible dimensions of differentiation in sub-systems. They are technology, territory and time. He states that

> Task performance is impaired if sub-systems within a system are differentiated along any other dimensions than these. However the basis of differentiation must not violate the task structure; boundaries should be so located as to associate each command with a whole task . . . Size by itself is not a critical factor.[1]

The notion of caring as a basis for the pastoral sub-system is too diffused to represent a 'whole' task, especially when the task of caring is that of all teachers.

Technology, or specialized skills and equipment, is clearly the basis of the curricular departmental sub-systems (as it is for intensive care, X-ray dapartments in hospitals and buying or personnel departments in stores and factories). Schools have long been accustomed to skill-based sub-systems. This may account, incidentally, for a fairly common assumption that the pastoral middle-management task involves special skills which are outside the training, experience and personal qualities of heads of department. In so far as experience makes anyone better at any job it may be true that skills of assessing and reporting are developed by house and year heads. It would, however, be sad if identification of their task with caring and welfare led to the assumption that they were experts in caring and welfare and that other teachers were excluded from these preoccupations.

A year system is based on year groups defined by age of pupils and the stages of the courses followed by the pupils in the year group. Similarly heads of lower, middle and upper school have their boundaries defined by the dimension of time (as do hospital departments for infants or geriatric patients, and factory or mine day and night shifts). Sometimes year systems are allocated their own territory in the school. A house system has no age/time boundary and therefore has greater need for territorial boundaries than a year system. Houses which lack territorial definition often go to great lengths to emphasize their separate identities by means of minor differentiation of uniform, badges, emblems,

[1] Rice, A. K., *The Enterprise and its Environment*, Tavistock Publications, 1963, p. 225.

mottoes, as well as the display cases of cups and shields which serve as the unit's household gods.

The two-tier structure of twenty-five years ago existed to gather together all the knowledge about pupils which was presented by subject teachers in partial, fragmented form, to make overall assessment of each pupil's progress in all his learning, to propose appropriate strategies where necessary in order to enable the pupil to learn more effectively, and to distribute this information to everyone concerned. It is probably true that these aims were rarely clearly stated and that form masters and mistresses saw little in their work beyond marking attendance registers and summarizing termly reports. In the small grammar or secondary-modern school it may often have been true, given the views about 'intelligence' prevalent then, that once the information was assembled about a pupil's progress, assessment was often superficial and measures to deal with the performance assessed were limited to promotion or demotion between streams or between types of schools. It remains true that however crude were the methods often then adopted, the purposes of the form system were directly related to pupils' learning: (1) collation of information about it; (2) assessing its strengths and weaknesses; (3) proposing measures to remedy its deficiencies; (4) distributing information and recommendations to pupils, parents, teachers, employers, admission authorities for higher education, and so on.

Such responsibilities are clearly directly related to the primary task of the school, which is the promotion of children's learning in the same way as a body plant, an engine shop or a paint shop are essential parts of a car factory.[1] Caring and welfare are not only parts of the functions of all the departments of the school but are also ancillary and supportive rather than the 'whole' tasks referred to by Miller.

The four functions listed above are all related, then, to the management of children's learning 'across the curriculum'. Despite frustrations, confusions and misunderstandings, this

---

[1] 'The following factors seem conducive to success — the pastoral organization is seen to support the school's prime purpose of learning. Whilst low achievement and poor motivation may have their causes in personal and social problems and need immediate solutions, a good curriculum, well taught, is also an agent of care. The divorce of academic and pastoral function may itself create difficulties by separating what is basically inseparable . . .' HMI Paper 'Conference on Comprehensive Education — Pastoral Care in Schools', 16 and 17 December 1977, Article 3, p. 6, para. 15.

is the function which most pastoral systems are expected to perform and in practice mostly do perform. With the movement towards the democratization of education, pupils and parents are increasingly informed and consulted. Assessments are conveyed more comprehensively and more comprehensibly, and 'consumerism' has ensured that the pupil and his parents play a greater part than hitherto in decision-making. These trends have increased the complexity of managing children's learning. They may indeed have arisen in part from the availability of a specialist sub-system to cope with them. The term 'guidance' is now used to refer to the whole process. The birth of the principle of guidance significantly coincides with the demise of the determination of pupils' educational and employment futures by the arbitrary means of the 11+ selection examination and by separate grammar and secondary-modern schools.

As with counselling, there is uncertainty in comprehensive schools about whether guidance skills of a sufficiently professional standard already exist in the pastoral system or whether guidance (particularly careers guidance) specialists are required who have undergone specific training. In any case a careers or guidance specialist cannot fulfil his role unaided with all the children of a large school. He or she therefore normally works through the pastoral system.

The general concept of 'guidance' is usually sub-divided into three parts — relationship, educational, and vocational. There is a close link between the personal and social development of a child, his choice of courses of study at school, and his eventual kind of employment. Pastoral systems generally are deeply involved in all three forms of guidance, with the specialized assistance often of a counsellor for the first aspect, a director of studies and sometimes the head of a remedial department for the second and a careers master or mistress for the third. Some management confusion sometimes arises from uncertainty about the relationship between the pastoral system and these three or four specialists. Probably the least satisfactory situation is one in which the responsibility for planning and providing the three forms of guidance resides with the specialists who 'use' the pastoral management system as their instrument. This situation places the pastoral middle manager in the position of being deprived of a clear management task, and the guidance specialists in the position of being managers without effective control over the means of implementing their responsibilities.

In discussing the nature of properly conceived roles in the last chapter, emphasis was placed upon the need for coherence, credibility and creativity. Management sub-systems require clear tasks which possess these three qualities. Pastoral systems have too often lacked a clear definition, and the term 'pastoral' (even more misleadingly 'pastoral care') has obscured the issues further. The most logical and helpful way forward is to recognize the actual contribution to the management of pupil learning which is performed by the existing 'pastoral' system and the guidance methods normally adopted, and to refer to this management system as the 'Guidance Organization' or 'Guidance Structure' of the school, defining its responsibilities in terms of relationship, educational and vocational guidance, with the four specific tasks of collation of information, assessment of learning, guidance for remedial action, and distribution of information. The teachers with specialized training in relationship counselling, in educational choice, in remedial provision and in careers information and advice and diagnosis of aptitude and interest would be designated as the providers of technical services to the managers and team members of the Guidance Organization.

For the sub-system, newly re-christened 'Guidance', to fulfil such responsibilities, class-contact time is required. In schools which have understood the pastoral system in terms of 'getting to know the pupils of your tutor group as individuals' and attending to their general welfare, a ten-minute session each morning to mark the register is often thought to be sufficient. Most of the teacher/pupil relationships are assumed to be developed during the breaks between lessons at mid-morning and lunch-time and during the morning assembly. Many schools have re-structured their time-tables to provide for an additional amount of tutor/tutor-group contact by a tutorial period once a week or once a fortnight. Vagueness about the objectives or primary task of the pastoral system has generally left house or year heads without a defined management task in relation to their tutors, and has left form tutors without a clear task in relation to their pupils. Conscientious tutors (and most tutors are extremely conscientious) have taken seriously the suggestion that their main task is to 'get to know their pupils individually'. Accordingly they have often devoted their tutorial sessions to personal interviews (either formal at the teacher's desk or informal as they move around the classroom) with individual pupils. While one pupil at a time may have derived considerable benefit from the interview the other twenty-nine in the normal group of thirty have frequently had insufficiently constructive pursuits to occupy their time. There are many complaints from form tutors themselves about card-playing and other leisure or non-educational activities during tutorial periods. Neither in initial training, nor in the leadership afforded in the pastoral system, has there been sufficient planning about the use of tutorial time. The fault lies not in the personalities of teachers in pastoral roles nor in their lack of commitment, but in an absence of clarity about the nature of their primary task.

If the primary task of pupils in schools is to learn and the role of pupils is defined as learning then the primary task of the pastoral or guidance system is to assist pupils to fulfil this role effectively. Such assistance is in itself a teaching task for teachers and a learning task for pupils. The first requisite for the fulfilment of this task is for teams of form tutors to agree about the content and approaches which are appropriate. For this to be possible the headmaster or headmistress must in the first instance make the necessary leadership available to the middle managers concerned. The leadership of the latter is, in its turn, necessary to provide form tutors with the stimulus and co-ordination which they require.

The idea of a 'pastoral curriculum or syllabus' is perhaps a strange one to teachers who have not thought of the objectives of the pastoral system as including any element of instruction or even any element of conscious learning. The idea of a 'guidance syllabus' (at least in its narrow interpretation of careers education) is more familiar.

If it is accepted that the role of the pastoral guidance system is to teach children how to become productive pupils, then the first item on its syllabus might well be explanation and discussion of the organization of the school, its geography and history, the roles of staff members, its rules and way of life, its facilities, needs and opportunities and its place in the local community. Pupils often seem to lack any clear view of the pattern of the curriculum to which they are subjected. A valuable increase in motivation might conceivably result from a survey of the learning experiences planned in the curriculum of a year group as well as of the reasons for the choice of material and approach which has been made. Pupils who at the beginning of a school year are handed a check-list of the knowledge and skills which they may hope to acquire in the next eleven months might be expected to look forward to the experiences in store with a positive attitude and might also be in a position at the end to assess the extent to which they had benefited from their schooling. As a by-product, the compilation of such a survey would be a valuable exercise in co-ordination for the teachers concerned and would enable them to work as a whole upon the children. The separate autonomy of curricular departments has remained virtually unchallenged in comprehensive schools in spite of the introduction of certain integrated courses, notably in the early secondary years in science and the humanities. It is significant that syllabuses are normally 'subject syllabuses', not year syllabuses. Consequently pastoral-guidance teachers are frequently largely ignorant of the learning which is expected of the pupils in their charge. Only in their own subject have they clear understanding. No doubt the production of year syllabuses is easier to suggest than to effect, not least because of the implication that in furnishing the information required, curricular departments are likely to feel they are constrained to surrender some of their independence and to defer to the needs of what is often regarded as a rival sub-system. The authority of the head to declare such a move to be school policy can only be acquired after the careful discussion of the purposes of the pastoral-guidance system in general and of year syllabuses in particular.

Year syllabuses, when they are compiled, are likely to reveal both gaps and anomalies. Many of the gaps and most of the anomalies can be rectified by the action of departments in amending their subject syllabuses. A thorough survey however of year syllabuses, involving a crosscheck with aims and objectives, will almost certainly show that many topics deemed important for pupil development and adaptation to future life are not included in the curriculum at all. Examination requirements cast their shadow well down the age-range below 16, and the examinations require so much factual knowledge that there is often room for little that is not to be examined. Though the first two or three years of a secondary course are relatively free from examination pressures, the children may be considered too young to be ready for the treatment of some important subjects. Some such topics do not clearly fall within the ambit of any subject department; others are subject-related but the subject concerned is an option which only certain pupils choose. When such topics have been identified and selected, it would seem that the pastoral-guidance organization (since it embraces all pupils) is the natural channel through which they should be treated. Careers and social education must obviously play an important part in the subjects chosen. Among many other subjects which a school staff might like to consider for inclusion in the pastoral curriculum (or at any rate use as a check-list to verify whether learning on such topics is already being provided for all children in the formal curriculum) are the following subjects:

road safety
safety on the water
first aid
sex education
education for parenthood
motor cycling
safety in the home
banking, money management and national savings
household budgeting
political education
countryside and wildlife preservation
computer education
racial equality
the EEC, the United Nations, the Third World
consumer education
alcohol, drugs and tobacco

Further choices might be made from among skills associated with what the school expects of its pupils, if such skills are not already among the specified objectives of curricular departments which minister to all pupils. These might include:

learning by heart
the presentation of written work
the planning of different kinds of written work
reading for different purposes
carrying and safeguarding books and equipment

The suggestion that the teaching of skills might form part of the work of the pastoral system poses the problem of how effective any teaching of skills can be when undertaken outside the context in which those skills would normally be used. Schools have sometimes instituted special courses in 'study skills', 'thinking' or 'health', for instance, because it was feared that what was everyone's responsibility might in practice prove to be no one's if responsibility for the work was widely diffused throughout the different subject departments and the whole staff group. Special courses are a comfort to those engaged in curriculum planning because they offer reassurance that specific provision has been made and you can actually point it out on the time-table. Such courses however have the disadvantage that the skills may need to be described in an abstract way and practised on tasks which do not arise naturally from the nature of the study itself but have to be artificially constructed for the sole purpose of exercising the skill concerned. In designing the objectives of a pastoral-guidance syllabus, the pastoral head and tutors would need to take this problem into account. In the end decisions about what the pastoral-guidance syllabus should include and what would be entrusted to specific departments must be made by individual schools in the light of what teachers consider will be most effective.

When the pastoral-guidance syllabus has been compiled and a suitable amount of class-contact time has been agreed, form tutors require preparation time and materials. This is an important responsibility for the house or year head. Teachers who are already hard-pressed in their roles as members of subject departments with heavy teaching loads as well as examination and homework marking, reports, correspondence with parents, games and out-of-school activities, may well feel that they have insufficient time left to prepare a pastoral-guidance syllabus. There is no doubt that the preparation will take considerable time in schools that have not hitherto adopted this approach. No school head should juggle the time-table to allow for extra

'tutorial periods' for 'next September' and expect everything to be ready in time. Three or four years ahead would
be a more realistic lapse of time between initial planning and
eventual implementation. The intervening time should
be devoted to in-service training designed to prepare teachers
for such a task. The 'problem-solving school' model of in-
service training, utilizing, in addition to its own resources,
the services of an LEA adviser, a teachers' centre warden,
and a college or university school of education lecturer in
the role of consultant might well be necessary before com-
mitting a school to such a pastoral-guidance teaching programme.

The advantages for the form tutors themselves in having
such a teaching programme in the school curriculum may
be significant in spite of the work required. Tutors, struggling
(as they often are) to 'get to know their pupils' in a vacuum
can get to know them much more effectively through the
medium of class teaching. Schools are, after all, institutions
based upon the class unit. School buildings consist mainly
of classrooms rather than private interview rooms. Schools
have the responsibility of supervising the orderly conduct of
their pupils and, in general, the time-table allocates between
twenty and thirty pupils to each teacher. The pupil/teacher
ratio does not permit individual, one-to-one, contacts except
at the cost of a much less favourable ratio elsewhere, or
at other times in the organization. Part of the problem
raised by the 'caring image' of 'pastoral care' has been the
assumption that it must adopt the methods as well as some
of the objectives of the social services. The staffing, facilities,
training and traditions of education are different
from those of the social services and schools will be more
successful in doing what they know how to do. If individual differences among pupils are important in the pastoral-
guidance relationship, they are equally important in the
curricular one. Subject teachers have traditionally found
ways of knowing and catering for individual needs. Opportunities for one-to-one conversations with children are
created by ensuring that the others are constructively occupied with learning work. A syllabus for form tutors enables
them to adopt the same tried methods.

The thesis of this chapter has been that, since comprehensive re-organization, the coherence of the school has
been adversely affected by the gulf which has grown between

the curricular and pastoral systems. Because of increased size and increased variety of curriculum, the power of the headmaster or headmistress to knit together the learning mediated by the departments was severely diminished. The pastoral system (or rather the middle management level in it) was set up to control the whole learning of the pupils relating to them as total human organisms rather than to the bits of them that were mathematicians, scientists, historians, geographers, artists, games players, craftsmen, users of language, and many others. It is unfortunate that, as time passed, the emphasis moved from learning to the human-relationships aspect of the original concept. The name 'pastoral care' may have had something to do with that. Similarly the importance of learning in the pastoral system may have been undermined by the early practice, when grammar and secondary-modern schools were combined in order to make one comprehensive school, of appointing the former grammar-school teachers, with their academic reputations, to be heads of subject departments, and the former secondary-modern heads of department, with their reputation for human understanding and tolerance, to be pastoral heads. The gulf between pastoral and curricular was often formally institutionalized in mixed schools with deputy heads of both sexes by placing the man in charge of the head of department system and the woman in charge of the pastoral system. The reciprocal wave effect of polarizing 'demanding' and 'caring' and of stereotyping the sexes has been mentioned in Chapter 5.

If the fragmentation in the school, in the pupil and in each individual teacher as he moves from fulfilling a curricular role into a pastoral one (two or three times a day) is to be replaced by greater coherence the first necessity is to re-define the objectives of the pastoral-guidance system in terms of learning. The second necessity is to re-specify the roles of the two deputies, man or woman, on dimensions other than pastoral and curricular. The third is to eliminate the practice of holding consultative meetings separately for curricular and pastoral/guidance middle managers. (Despite the problem of establishing agenda which concern the one but not the other, heads have often felt obliged to arrange separate consultative meetings in order to reduce the number attending to manageable proportions — there are normally far more curricular heads of department than there are pastoral heads.) The grouping of subjects into 'Faculties' has been a development arising largely, though not entirely, from this need.[1]

The fourth measure which may be helpful in bringing together the two management systems in a common sense of purpose is to establish specialist faculty/departmental rooms for all principal areas of the curriculum in the territorial area occupied by the pastoral unit. In this way pupils can be taught in their pastoral area instead of associating it solely with cloakrooms, registration, morning assembly, break, dinner time and leisure activities. It must be admitted that this can be done only at the expense of decentralizing specialized departmental equipment and materials. This is unlikely to be popular with heads of departments and may even be impossible for such departments as science, crafts and physical education.

The fifth measure which can be explored is to try to ensure that subject teaching and tutorial pastoral responsibilities bring the same teachers and pupils together to the greatest possible extent. Clearly there are also problems connected with this suggestion since it may be impossible to allocate a middle-school tutor group to a teacher whose subject is taught only in the fourth- and fifth-year option scheme, and women PE teachers may never teach the boys in their tutor groups as they may never teach any boys at all. The reverse may apply to men PE teachers. Value-judgements and priorities are involved in decisions about the allocation of tutor groups and subject classes and each school has to consider its own most pressing needs.

---

[1] 'One argument for faculties is purely organizational. Decision making by heads alone is giving place to healthier participation and in consequence many schools have set up planning bodies of various kinds. Frequently the desire both to keep such bodies manageably small and to ensure that the academic and pastoral sides are balanced requires the academic side to be represented by far fewer than 12 to 15 heads of traditional departments. A faculty structure fits this purpose readily but if that is the sole or main reason for its introduction it is a clear case of the organizational tail wagging the curricular dog.'

HMI Paper 'Conference on Comprehensive Education — Internal Organisation', 16 and 17 December 1977.

I accept that 'Faculty Heads' need to be truly representative of the subject areas for which they are responsible, if they are to have authority to speak for those areas in consultation. However there is no obligation for such an organizational restructuring to affect the curriculum unless this is desired for other purposes. In other words the organizational tail belongs to the consultative dog rather than the curricular one.

Finally there may be some value in discussing the rival claims of the 'house' (vertical) and the 'year' (horizontal) systems. Most of the advantages and disadvantages claimed in the early, now largely defunct, controversy proved to be emotional and lacked rational justification. The good example of some responsible senior pupils, claimed as an advantage for the house system, can be offset by the bad example of irresponsible senior pupils. The allegedly greater affinity of children for others of their own age (claimed as an advantage of the year system) is plainly untrue for adolescent girls, who prefer the company of older boys. Continuity of pupil and parent contact with the same house staff can equally well be afforded by the year system. Indeed five- or seven-year continuity is arguably a mixed blessing.

Perhaps the most important point to note (as Michael Marland remarks in *Pastoral Care*[1]) is that most schools, in fact, have both house and year systems. Few Physical Education departments can select teams to compete against one another without the facility of vertical teams or houses which provide both players and supporters. Schools organize the curriculum on a year basis and it is rare for classes to contain more than a twelve-month age-range, though occasionally 'family style' tutor groups are organized in this way. The house-based pastoral system has merely selected the competitive team organization to be its basis, while the year-based pastoral system selects the curricular system as its basis. The house system tends to widen the gulf between pastoral and curricular since curricular decisions have to be taken outside the system. The year system tends to emphasize the separation of pupils of different ages. Whichever system exists or is adopted it is desirable to foster activities either *across* the age-group or *between* year groups to offset the separations which each creates.

---

[1] Marland, M., *Pastoral Care*, Heinemann, 1974.

7 Participation and Consultation

In the section of Chapter 5 concerning the role of the head-master or headmistress it was suggested as a useful hypothesis that an important, perhaps its most important responsibility is to develop the skills and understanding of the teaching staff. Consultation and participation were stated to be the main means by which this purpose could be promoted. In schools, which are institutions dedicated to the growth and self-fulfil-ment of pupils, it should not be necessary to argue the case for the growth and self-fulfilment of teachers. If theoretical justification were needed, it is furnished by Maslow's hierarchy of needs.[1] He suggested that human needs may be classified in a rank order of urgency from physiological, through safety, social and ego needs to self-fulfilment. When needs for food, drink, sleep, protection, security, acceptance, recognition and self-esteem have been satisfied, people seek creativity and self-realization. It seems probable that, for teachers, physiological, safety, social and ego needs are normally met in sufficient measure for a conscious seeking after self-fulfilment to be commonly apparent. (Where it is *not* apparent, perhaps the more urgent needs, lower in the hierarchy, may be too press-ing. Reluctance to take part in consultative processes may be a danger signal which management should heed!).

There are other reasons why there is a marked shift from authoritarian modes of leadership to a more consultative one.

1. The move is considered to be 'democratic' and consistent with the spirit of the age.
2. It is considered to be a more effective strategy for bringing about changes which require a re-orientation of people's beliefs rather than merely the adoption of a different routine practice.

[1] Maslow, A. H., *Motivation and Personality*, Harper & Row, 1970.

In industry and commerce, the participation movement started several decades ago. Writing in 1960, McGregor in *The Human Side of Enterprise* (Chapters 3 and 4)[1], described the authoritarian assumptions of management as 'Theory X' and analysed them; he entitled 'Theory Y' the characteristic assumptions of a participatory form of management. The expectations of the general public are that heads of schools should be authoritarian leaders in many aspects of their roles; indeed approval is often expressed for heads who coerce and control by the use of power. No doubt the relative slowness with which there has developed a readiness to expect participation in schools is connected with reluctance by an older generation to trust the judgement of a younger generation. Schools are perceived as institutions entrusted with the *control* of young people. Management styles tend to reflect each other at different levels, so that what is deemed good for teacher/pupil relations tends to be expected in head/staff relations too. When the predominant feeling (ascendant though by no means exclusive or unchallenged) is that teachers should manage children arbitrarily and coercively (what else is the clamour for greater 'discipline' about?) there is a momentum for a similar style to be considered natural at middle and top management level. A certain tension has resulted in schools between this momentum and the participatory one found in nearly every other kind of institution. In spite of the difficulties, the participatory movement is a powerful one and is accepted in most schools as desirable. In 'Leadership and Decision-Making in Education'[2], Professor Hoyle develops two models of organizations (A and B). Of Model B (the participatory one) he says

> Generally speaking, greater moral value and practical efficiency has been attributed to concepts of organization which approximate to Model B; . . . its democratic structure and support for self-actualisation amongst participants is congruent with the prevailing Weltanschaung.

Democracy and practical efficiency are not often considered to be highly compatible. Dictators, rather than committees, are normally supposed to get things done, whatever their other shortcomings. Apologists for Mussolini used to point with approval to the fact that Italian trains ran to time

[1] McGregor, D., *The Human Side of Enterprise*, McGraw-Hill, 1960.
[2] Hughes, M. (ed.), *Administering Education: International Challenge*, Athlone Press, 1975, pp. 31, 32.

under the Fascist regime. In coercive organizations, where severe penalties exist, it is always possible to ensure that there is general compliance with clear explicit instructions, the breach of which can be detected swiftly and certainly. However, all organizations also require the broad assent of their members since responsible initiative is only taken by subordinates who are animated by a degree of zeal for the objectives of the regime. In Nazi Germany and Fascist Italy much effort was devoted through propaganda promises and mass rallies to stimulating fervour for the causes of the dictatorships.

Schools too make use of certain coercive powers and of corporate rituals to force or enlist the support of their members. These means are nevertheless rarely sufficient or philosophically approved. Since implicit in most concepts of education in Western civilization is the idea of the autonomy of the individual and his freedom to choose the way he will develop, a greater degree of participation (at least among the more adult members) tends to be taken for granted.[1] Neither coercion nor indoctrination is appropriate in a system which aims at personal autonomy for its members.

In the Open University's Course E283, Units 4–5, 'The Management of Innovation in Schools' (1972), Bolam and Pratt explain the three principal strategies originally identified by Chin and Benne[2]:

1. In the case of power-coercive strategies, people or groups lower in a hierarchical system respond to those higher up because, if they do not, sanctions may be involved; they may be coerced; they are in this sense, responding to power whether it is latent or manifest. 'Advice' is perceived as non-rejectable, i.e. as an order.

---

[1] In *Education for Personal Autonomy*, British Association for Counselling: Bedford Square Press, 1978, H. J. Blackham traces this concept back to its origins in Athenian culture. He quotes R. F. Dearden's definition: 'A person is autonomous to the degree that what he thinks and does in the more important areas of his life cannot be explained without reference to his own activity of mind.'

Dearden, R. F., 'Autonomy and Education', in Dearden, R. F., Hirst, P. H. and Peters, R. S. (eds.), *Education and the Development of Reason*, Routledge & Kegan Paul, 1972.

[2] Chin, R. and Benne, K. D., 'General Strategies for Effecting Change in Human Systems' in Bennis, W., Benne, K. D. and Chin, R., *The Planning of Change*, Holt, Rinehart & Winston, 1970.

2. In the case of rational-empirical strategies, the 'change agent' appeals to the enlightened self interest of the group or of the 'client'. With shared premises established, it is the force of logical argument that is expected to prevail.

3. In the case of normative-re-educative strategies where, as Bolam put it (in his Reader article) 'effective innovation requires a change of attitudes, relations, values and skills and, therefore, the activation of forces within the client system' shared premises clearly cannot be assumed. So (unless coercive power is to be used to tell the client what to think and feel!) there must be some approach made to the identification of common ground from which action can spring.[1]

The problems confronting schools which are seeking to change in the face of changing needs are nearly all of the kind which demand changes in 'attitudes, relations, values and skills'. The 'normative-re-educative strategy' is therefore the appropriate one. Many of the problems even imply profound reappraisal of the existing conscious or unconscious assumptions of the members regarding the aims, objectives or basic purposes for which the school exists. There may well be personal biases and preferences in the mind of the head but there can be no certainty. Consultation using a 'normative-re-educative strategy' should be regarded as normative and re-educative for all those participating — whatever may be their roles in the management hierarchy.

Bolam and Pratt emphasize the *efficacy* of the normative-re-educative strategy with this example:

> There are many important problems which meet with an impasse when the manager of change has only power-coercive strategies at his disposal. To instruct the staff of a school to change over to mixed ability teaching is, at best, likely to result only in a limited 'mechanical' conformity with the directive, since some if not all of the staff are likely to respond by playing safe — they comply only with the 'letter of the law'; at worst it is to invite them to ignore the directive altogether, or even to defy it.[2]

Philip Sadler, Principal of Ashridge Management College, reviews the work of R. Tannenbaum and W. H. Schmidt in a *New Society* article[3]. In 'How to choose a leadership

[1] Bolam, R. and Pratt, S., op. cit., pp. 16, 17.

[2] op. cit., p. 19.

[3] Sadler, P., 'Leadership Styles in Flux', in *New Society*, Vol. 21, No. 520, pp. 546-8, 21. 9. 1972.

pattern' in the *Harvard Business Review* they distinguished four specific styles:

1. the Tells Style;
2. the Sells Style;
3. the Consults Style;
4. the Joins Style.

They define these as follows:

> The manager who employs the 'Tells' style habitually makes his own decisions and announces them to his subordinates expecting them to carry these out without question.

> The manager who uses the 'Sells' approach also makes his own decisions, but rather than simply announce them to his subordinates, he tries to persuade them to accept his decision. Recognizing the possibility of resistance, he attempts to reduce it by salesmanship.

> The manager who uses the 'Consults' style does not make his decision until he has presented the problem to members of the group and listened to their advice and suggestions. The decision is still his but he does not take it until after he has consulted his staff.

> The 'Joins' style involves delegating to the group (which includes the manager himself as a member), the right to make decisions. The manager limits himself to defining the problem. The decision reflects the opinion of the majority of the group.

Tannenbaum and Schmidt went on to compare, in the Ashridge Management College Research Project, the correlation of subordinates' perception of leadership styles with the manner in which they perceived the behaviour of their manager in a range of aspects. The consultative leader scored significantly higher than other types on all aspects of behaviour.

The persuasive 'salesman' type was the next in order of preference. The only type, if type it can be called, who was below average on all counts was the manager with no detectable style at all. Presumably this type fluctuates unpredictably from one style or strategy to another.

In practice most heads of schools do differentiate between 'routine' matters, which clearly fall within generally agreed policies, and 'new' questions, which raise issues not previously agreed. In the first category would come decisions concerning the school calendar, the implementation of school rules and practice, and of all the accepted procedures concerning reports, the admission of new pupils, the appointment of staff and similar routine. It would be normal for a head or a deputy head to take executive action on such matters without it being supposed that consultation was necessary or desirable. If, however, a head thought that any of the established procedures, such as those mentioned, needed changing, it is now less likely that he would take unilateral action. Since such changes affect 'attitudes, relations, values and skills', he would be well advised to adopt the 'normative-re-educative' strategy. He would place before his colleagues a statement of why he thought present procedures were falling short and listen to opinions. Under such a leadership style it would, of course, be equally open to any other members to initiate a re-examination of existing procedures.

Though a head may adopt more than one style, his choice should be predictable. When the members of a group cannot foretell how a problem is likely to be approached, the expectations of at least some will be frustrated, and the result will be dissatisfaction and confusion.

The move by a head towards consultative procedures is not necessarily whole-heartedly approved or understood even by those who are members of the management of the school, that is, the teachers; still less may the general public understand. There is a common readiness to equate leadership with the 'power-coercive' or authoritarian mode of action. Efforts to improve participation may well be unwelcome and interpreted as weakness or abdication of leadership. It may also be advisable to remember Maslow's 'hierarchy of needs' referred to earlier. If teachers are exhausted or feel insecure, unaccepted or unrecognized, they will be impatient with proposals that they should assume more burdens in the interests of their personal development. They should not be condemned for this very natural sense of priorities. It is the responsibility of management to look for such reasons and to try to remedy conditions.

Opposition to participation is frequently attributed to personality characteristics of individual members. School staffs are divided in some accounts into two categories, the participators and the non-participators. Thus Arnold Jennings in 'The Participation of the Teaching Staff in Decision-Making in Schools' writes:

Many examples can soon be found in schools, probably none of them very large schools, that come fairly close to [benevolent despotism] and in which the staff are very ready to accept this mode of working. There are very many teachers in schools who do *not* thirst to share in, or to take over, responsibility and are only too pleased that responsibility lies on someone else and not on them, and are very content to go straight home at the end of afternoon school and let someone else wrestle with some problem, and announce the decision next day. Whether they should be looked down on for this, or whether it is our duty to stir up in them a divine discontent with such methods, very many teachers do take this attitude. This is a fact that is often ignored, and it should not be.[1]

Jennings, of course, also recognized another kind of teacher — 'there are very many indeed who wish to have some share in making at least some of the decisions (and others who wish for much more than this)'.

Similarly Strauss ('Some Notes on Power Equalisation')[2] is interpreted by Bolam and Pratt (op. cit.) as saying that 'many people prefer the security of a traditional hierarchic non-participative structure and are very reluctant to assume the responsibility that power-sharing throws upon them'.

The recognition of these differing reactions to participation leads to a number of suggestions about how to deal with the problem. Jennings expressed his uncertainty about whether to disapprove of those who are happy with a despotism or whether to try to stir them into participation. Bolam and Pratt consider the need to 'discover a significant set of instances in which it is rational to use a control strategy, even if it might be best re-labelled "power-submissive" or perhaps "power-collusive".' They agree that this may well be disturbing or even unacceptable to some. 'However', they go on to comment, 'it does appear to correspond with "the facts" as we see them and it also points to a potentially fruitful area for further investigation.' The significant phrase is ' "the facts" as we see them', since the same phenomena are capable of different interpretations.

In all the quoted comments the reluctance to participate, noted as a 'factual' behavioural feature, is deemed to be a

---

[1] Jennings, A., 'The Participation of the Teaching Staff in Decision-Making in Schools' in Andrews, P. and Parkes, D. (eds.), *Participation, Accountability and Decision-Making at Institutional Level*, Proceedings of the Third Annual Conference of the British Educational Administration Society, Coombe Lodge, Blagdon, Bristol, 1975, p. 28.

[2] Stauss, G., 'Some Notes on Power Equalisation in Carver, F.D. and Sergiovanni, T. J., *Organizations and Human Behaviour, Focus on Schools*, McGraw-Hill, 1969.

personality trait, integral to character and hence fundamentally unalterable (though stimulation of 'divine discontent' might be attempted). Presumably coercion might be
attempted, but this is recognized as likely to result in only
mechanical compliance.

Writers about leadership and management frequently
seem to conduct a logical argument about the need for
participation only to reach the eventual point of defeat
that some people just do not want to be involved. Then
there seems to be no way forward. The two alternative
strategies of accepting the situation or employing sanctions
or 'non-rejectable advice' to obtain at least token attendance
at meetings are obviously both equally unsatisfactory. The
logic of the impasse stems from an assumption about 'taking
people as they are'. It is based upon a view of human personality as inert rather than dynamic, isolated rather than
inter-reactive.

Elizabeth Richardson[1] suggests that the ideas of Melanie
Klein[2] offer a very different and more fruitful perspective.
Elizabeth Richardson writes:

> The important thing is that persons in the group are liable to be
> used by the group to contain and perhaps also to express aspects
> of other persons. This process of projection and introjection can
> be either helpful to growth and to the work of the group or inimical
> to it. What we are looking at here is, according to Melanie Klein and
> others who have built on her ideas, a very primitive mechanism that
> begins in infancy and continues throughout our lives — the mechan-
> ism that enables us to handle conflict within ourselves by splitting
> off our good and bad feelings and putting them out, as fantasied
> 'good objects' and 'bad objects', into other people . . . Examples
> of the adult use of these unconscious mechanisms are not hard to
> find. As teachers we have all made use of them. If, for example,
> the ultra-conservative aspects of ourselves can be pushed out into
> parents, or employers, or local administrators, or the government,
> or perhaps into certain well-established members of the school
> staff itself, most of us can avoid looking at our own fears of change
> and deny our own wish to keep things comfortably as they are.[3]

She goes on to point out that the same mechanism enables us
to saddle teacher-trainers, educational researchers and innova-
tors among our own colleagues with our own ultra-liberalism
and so avoid acceptance of our own rebelliousness and 'deny
our impatience with the establishment'.

---

[1] Richardson, E., *The Teacher, the School and the Task of Management*,
Heinemann, 1973.
[2] Klein, M., *Our Adult World and its Roots in Infancy*, Heinemann, 1963.
[3] op. cit., p. 27.

Fig. 2 Projection and introjection

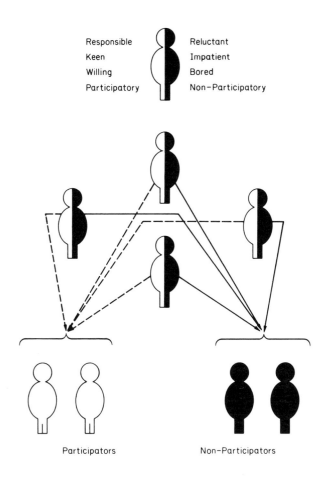

Responsible — Reluctant
Keen — Impatient
Willing — Bored
Participatory — Non-Participatory

Participators   Non-Participators

This may be the mechanism which divides staff groups into participators and non-participators. Is it not more fruitful, instead, to recognize that *all* teachers want to take part in the management of the school responsibly and that the *same* teachers are bored with the process and are reluctant to devote the time required? Such a recognition entails taking back into ourselves either the enthusiasm or the boredom, the eagerness or the reluctance which we have projected into other individuals. It results in a resumption of the inner conflict and is therefore sometimes painful.

This process of recognition is described by Elizabeth Richardson.

> If we carry the idea into the educational field it becomes possible to perceive the teacher in relation to pupils and the head (and other senior staff members) in relation to staff as having a 'holding' or 'containing' function that enables the individual, in time, to take back his own violent and potentially overwhelming feelings and work at the problem of understanding them.

The lesson for a head and senior staff members is to avoid colluding with the assumption that some staff members are non-participatory and therefore 'bad' and others are participatory and therefore 'good'. The 'holding' or 'containing' function is to withhold praise or blame from either reaction but to work positively with the staff group towards a recognition of the co-existence within each member (including the top management members themselves) of ambivalent and conflicting feelings about participation and consultation.

In *Running a School*, Barry and Tye[1], like Jennings and others, face the problem of teachers who would rather go home at the end of afternoon school and declare a lack of interest in taking part in staff meetings. They suggest that a head should make some meetings mandatory and declare others to be voluntary. This of course places upon the head the right and duty to coerce teachers (perhaps by non-rejectable advice) to attend meetings which he considers important and to excuse them from those which are less important. There are many objections to such a procedure. It is a highly dubious assumption that it is appropriate to use any form of coercion, however gentle and well meant, for the purpose of ensuring participation, or that it would be effective in procuring more than physical presence if it were complied with at all. It is destructive of the very power-sharing (or at least influence-sharing) it is meant to encourage. Coercion implies that attendance of subordinates is required to minister to the needs of the head, and excusing attendance implies

---

[1] Barry, C. H. and Tye, F. *Running a School*, Maurice Temple Smith, 1972.

both that participation is unnecessary (and indeed valueless) and that the non-attender need feel no guilt at the choice he or she has made. There are many occasions when a teacher is faced with a difficult decision between two equally important obligations. Even though dates of staff meetings may have been programmed well in advance (as they should be), other outside obligations frequently clash. These other commitments may be anything from a child's birthday party or a wedding anniversary party to an in-service training course. The guilt which a teacher is bound to feel at missing an outside duty of this kind (not all duties are unpleasant) is no smaller than the guilt he will feel at missing a staff meeting. The obligation to choose is individual and inalienable from a teacher's status as a mature adult. A head who takes it upon himself to 'excuse' a teacher from a staff meeting is suggesting that the obligation to participate in the management of the school is one which is owed to the head personally, since no one can exonerate another from obligations owed to third parties. It may be said that 'excusing' attendance or making it voluntary is merely an indication that the meeting is unimportant. If that is so, one wonders whether it should be called at all. If, on the other hand, a head refuses to 'excuse' attendance at a meeting he is assuming an omnipotence and an omniscience which he does not possess. In effect he is accepting responsibility for excusing the teacher from a conflicting responsibility at home, or on a course for which he is enrolled. This responsibility belongs, properly, not to the head, but to the teacher himself or herself.

It was suggested that teachers feel guilt at missing staff meetings, however unavoidably. They will not do so if the meetings serve no purpose that they can detect other than suiting the head's convenience. A properly conceived meeting should promote the learning and understanding of those who take part. Each member, therefore, is under an obligation to himself or herself. Since properly organized meetings are discussions (information can be more effectively conveyed on paper), every contribution is valuable. We clarify our ideas about issues through hearing and supporting or challenging the opinions of others and by having our own opinions heard, supported or challenged by others. Our presence, therefore, and the contribution we make is an obligation we owe to the learning of our colleagues. Since the issues which ought to be the subject of staff meetings are issues of insti-

tutional management, teachers, as people who on appointment have accepted a role as members of the school internal
management, owe an obligation to the school institution
and to the teaching profession. It must be reiterated that
these three obligations to oneself, to one's colleagues and to
the school do not lie within a head's jurisdiction. The responsibility of the head is not to force participation or to excuse
non-participation but to clarify the nature of the obligations
involved. This is not to say that attendance or absence need
be haphazard, unnoticed or unpredictable. Teachers who are
clear in their minds about the three obligations and decide
on a particular occasion that an outside commitment has
priority, should accept their own personal loss and express
through the head their apologies to their colleagues as learning
individuals and as members of the school management group.
In practice members of a group can rapidly acquire this
outlook and behave in this way.

The particular analysis attempted here of the management
responsibility of teachers will not be universally accepted.
The pressures upon teachers' time and nervous energy which
have developed in recent years coincide with mounting criticism of the effectiveness of education. Thus teachers find
themselves working harder than ever before with diminished
recognition and lowered morale. It is not surprising that
teachers are increasingly rebellious when resources are
threatened, salary increases are grudged, their work is so
often undervalued and they are expected to raise standards,
halt pollution and social decadence, re-shape curriculum
and methods, examine, evaluate, revivify the surrounding
community, participate in parent/teacher social events,
run extra-curricular activities, take part in in-service training
and also participate in the management of the school. The
combination of mounting criticism and vastly increased
responsibilities is a volatile mixture which can only be
made safe by a removal of one of the two ingredients if an
unfortunate chemical reaction is not to ensue. The preference of most teachers would be for a diminution of critical
dissatisfaction and its replacement by public recognition
that all the ills of our society cannot be laid at the door of
our schools and that much of the good which we see around
us can. It would be more profitable for critics, especially
those in the media, to consider their responsibility for
social ills and how much worse these might be without the

education service. Although James Callaghan in his Ruskin speech and the Green Paper on education refused to blame teachers for everything, too many other influential voices regard everything from crime statistics to the state of the economy as the responsibility of schools. There appear to many educationists to be insurmountable difficulties in the way of convincing the nation that 'it is not our fault'. Consequently some teachers' unions are tackling the other ingredient in the mixture — the ever-increasing demands upon teachers' time. This move takes the form of pressing local education authorities to define what is 'contractual' and what is 'voluntary'. Clearly the origin of this demand is in the lack of recognition which society at present accords to the efforts of teachers rather than in a wish to avoid certain duties and responsibilities. The evidence for this is that certain teachers' unions have recently advised their members temporarily not to participate in certain activities such as parents' meetings and staff meetings out of school time, in order to demonstrate the extent to which the education service depends upon the voluntary goodwill of teachers.

In fact the effort to distinguish between 'contractual' and 'voluntary' activities is ill-advised and, if successful, could only lead to a down-grading of teaching from being a 'professional' activity. There are no easy criteria by which anyone could judge what should be 'contractual'. Attendance in front of time-tabled classes or on the school premises during school hours is both insufficient, and too much; insufficient as it leaves wide open the question of what a teacher does when he is there, and stipulates no obligation to prepare lessons or mark books; too much, as in well-conducted schools teachers are usually able to leave the school premises whenever they are not teaching, deciding on their own responsibility that they are fulfilling the needs of their task thereby; similarly teachers engaged in team teaching or within a faculty time-table should be free to re-structure the time-table to meet the children's needs and those of the course.

The purpose of a school is clearly to promote the whole field of children's learning as a means of enabling them to increase their mastery over their present and future experiences. The role of the teacher is to manage the experiences of children in such a way that useful learning takes place.

This is an open-ended brief. Although local education authorities have in most cases laid down the minimum number of hours during which a school shall be open (and DES regulations lay down the minimum number of school sessions in a year) these regulations were never intended to be regarded as a maximum, nor did anyone, least of all teachers themselves, expect that this number of hours and sessions would ever be a maximum in practice in any school. The professional part of being a teacher as an individual, and of being a member of a service, is that teachers can examine for themselves as individuals and corporately as a staff group in any given school what they can offer beyond the minimum. They will take into account the needs of the children and of the school and balance them against the diminishing returns resulting from progressive exhaustion. Recognition by local education authorities, as the elected representatives of each community, of the incalculable value of what teachers do, way beyond the minimum requirements, is long overdue. However, this is very different from the suggestion made by some teachers that a distinction by LEAs between voluntary and contractual can either free teachers to opt out of the voluntary activities or coerce them effectively into engaging in the contractual activities. As with the relationship of heads with their colleagues about participating in the management of the school, so is the relationship of LEAs with teachers about the wide responsibilities of being a member of the teaching profession. They have neither the right to coerce nor the prerogative to exonerate. Society should interpret the move rightly as a request for overdue recognition and respond accordingly both at local and national levels; but LEAs would do a lasting disservice to teachers, to themselves and to the public if they tried to answer the question in the terms in which it is being posed by some teachers' unions.

The responsibility to participate in the management of a school is, therefore, one which is inherent today in the nature of being a teacher. It cannot be eliminated by some kind of professional absolution by a head or remission by a local education authority. 'Mandatory', 'optional', 'contractual' and 'voluntary' are words which belong to the vocabulary of a totally different set of circumstances. Questions which offer alternatives between either word in each pair are traps of the 'Have you stopped beating your wife? —

Answer yes or no!' variety. It is easy to understand that teachers are beset by uncertainty on this question. They can point to the fact that some heads set up consultative machinery, while others do not. Moreover until comparatively recently there was no such opportunity for participation nor such expectation. How then can the obligation be inherent? It is true that it was not even present in the expectations which governed the teaching role only a few years ago. Then the purposes and methods of schools were widely recognized, simple and pre-determined (though rarely articulated). Now they are problematic, complex and subject to widely differing local needs both inside the school and in the community which it serves. Then schools could rely on tradition; now the pace of change is breathtaking. Then teachers were trained for life at the age of 21 or 22; now they need constant self re-training until they retire. Moreover, as Jennings writes, 'there is the impact in this sphere [participation] of one of the great secular trends of the world to-day . . . in a dozen spheres people are not prepared to accept something as on authority, as a generation ago they would have done.'[1] Although there is, in all teachers, a side to their minds which regrets these developments and looks back to a golden age (whether they personally experienced it or only heard about it from the old-timers), in fact, there is no putting the clock back. Teaching now involves taking part in management.

As this responsibility is a quite recent development, there is no tried and proved tradition about how it should be shouldered. Schools which recognize the need for staff participation (most but perhaps not all) present a picture of very great variety in experimental methods adopted to bring it about.

The problem of the large staff meeting

The most obvious device for consulting the teaching staff and involving its members in the management of the school is the 'Staff Meeting'. Some may see no problem in con-

[1] Jennings, A., 'The Participation of the Teaching Staff in Decision-Making in Schools', *Participation, Accountability and Decision-Making at Institutional Level*, Proceedings of the Third Annual Conference of the British Educational Administration Society, Coombe Lodge, Blagdon, Bristol, 1975.

vening the whole staff, presenting it with specific proposals and encouraging members to vote for or against each proposal. Policies might, at first sight, be satisfactorily determined in this way. Others might object that, in present-day conditions, the large numbers of teachers which a full meeting comprises, the complexity of the issues, the divergence of views likely to exist and the accountability of the head, pose considerable problems for this kind of Athenian democracy.

Elizabeth Richardson describes these problems:

> Such rapid expansion [in the number of teachers] creates for a headmaster a dilemma about how best to use the resources within his staff group in the actual process of policy formation. Some heads give up having staff meetings when size becomes 'unmanageable'; others persevere, though with growing doubts about their efficacy.[1]

and

> To some, the apparently simple process of taking a vote on any controversial issue — a vote which would be binding on the headmaster — appeared to be the obvious solution in moments of conflict and disagreement. But when matters of real importance to the school were at stake, the taking of a vote did not recommend itself to him (the head) at all, since this would have inevitably left in the staff group dissatisfied, over-ruled minority groups that could hardly have been expected to work whole-heartedly to implement decisions enforced by the majority.

It is not now uncommon for the staff group of a school to number anything from 70 to 120 members. Heads may well feel themselves reluctant to face such a large gathering of professional colleagues. Indeed, if discontent or criticism is felt to any significant extent by a staff group a confrontation of 70 or more with one can be an intimidating experience for the one. Probably few heads would admit to being terrified of the collective strength of a school staff; headmasters and headmistresses are expected to be terrifying rather than terrified; an admission of apprehension is likely to be considered tantamount to an admission of inadequacy. If schools cease to hold full meetings of the entire staff, there are valid reasons too for questioning the efficacy of such meetings. Only a minority of members are likely to get a chance to

[1] Richardson, E., *The Teacher, the School and the Task of Management*, Heinemann, 1973, p. 153.

speak; sometimes only the school hall is large enough to seat all the members. In other schools it is felt that the interests and responsibilities of the staff are so diverse that members can have little common ground on which to base constructive discussion.

It seems probable that few schools totally abolish opportunities for the entire staff to meet together. The inherent threat of such a large gathering and some of the other problems may be met by stipulating a purely social purpose such as an end-of-term sherry party when the relaxed and fatigued assembly is unlikely to raise hostile or controversial issues. In other schools a full staff meeting is only called to listen passively to information communicated by the head and deputies or to receive exhortations to behave in a way which the top management considers desirable. When full staff meetings are reserved for social occasions or for exhortations, those in leadership positions provide for themselves an effective protection against the potential threat of the large meeting.

It would be unfair to heads to imply that the large meeting is a threat only to them. Equally, ordinary staff members experience such a meeting similarly. Perhaps the apprehension is most acute for the most senior staff members (the quality of whose leadership may well be questioned), and for the youngest and least experienced (who may feel disqualified from making an acceptable contribution). The heads of department, of houses or year groups are least likely to understand or sympathize with the anxieties of those senior or junior to them. 'Middle managers' have their promotion and their experience to give them a degree of security; they have a sense of solidarity with and support from other heads of department or pastoral heads; moreover their roles do not entail responsibility for more than a sector of the school's task and do not consequently expose them to the likelihood of general criticism from their colleagues.

It might therefore be expected that full staff meetings are desired more by those in middle management and less by those in the most senior and the most junior roles. In spite, nevertheless, of their reservations heads tend to be conscious of the need for consultation in which all the teachers can take part, and most young teachers who have just completed their initial training generally have a wish to see their new perspectives, fresh ideas and energetic

enthusiasm engaged in some way which will enable their
influence to be felt.

Permanent and temporary systems as a basis for consultation

Since the major objection to the full staff meeting as a basis
for consultation is its size, it might be thought reasonable to
break down the full group into its constituent parts, which
are the sub-systems comprising the formal structure of
responsibility. Departmental or faculty meetings are certain
to be held in any case. Similarly there will be meetings of the
tutors of a house or year group. It would seem a possible
solution to ask these existing groups to devote some of
their meetings or some parts of their meetings to the discussion of issues important to the whole school. In practice the
identification (with their specialist subject disciplines) of
teachers meeting as members of a department tends to make
this unpopular. Such a proposal also limits each member's
contact with others teaching different ingredients in the
curriculum. Consequently the cross-fertilization which staff
meetings ought to offer is precluded by the use of departmental meetings as a means of consultation on whole-school
policies.

If the apparent 'narrowness' of subject specialisms is an
objection to departmental meetings for this purpose, it would
seem that pastoral groupings do not suffer from this disadvantage. House or year form tutors are usually drawn from
many different departments. An experimental use of meetings
of the tutors of the 'lower school' (years 1 and 2), the 'middle
school' (years 3, 4 and 5) and the 'upper school' (the lower
and upper sixth) as organs for consultation on general school
policy proved unacceptable to the teachers concerned on the
grounds that they did not wish to be narrowly identified
with the interests and viewpoint of a limited age-range of
pupils out of the whole 11–18 span for which the school
catered. They pointed out that, though they might be first-
year tutors, they also taught in the sixth form, and upper
school tutors also taught in the younger year-groups. In fact
the disadvantages of this way of constructing smaller groups
were similar to those arising if departmental meetings were
used to serve the same purpose.

The disadvantages of consulting through smaller units of
the permanent, formal staff structure have led to experi-

ments with small groups that are unrelated to the formal structure, or only loosely associated with it. Most of these have a greater degree of impermanence than the formal structure. Such groups are often favoured because, as 'temporary systems' (see reference in Chapter 2, p. 14, to Miles 'On Temporary Systems') they tend to facilitate change by contributing to the 'organic' nature of the institution. Departments and house/year systems are part of the permanent, hierarchic system. While the permanent systems are essential for the maintenance of the organization, they are possibly slower to propose changes. There may, however, be other reasons why teachers often favour 'temporary systems' (in spite of the fact that their impermanence and lack of status makes them apter to *propose* changes than to *implement* them). Elizabeth Richardson observed:

> There is among teachers a wide-spread fear that to accept the reality that different levels of skill and responsibility exist and must be reflected in the management structure implies accepting a diminution of their own power to influence decisions taken by the head. The existence of a hierarchy (which is, in fact, an ordering of tasks and responsibilities) is seen as undemocratic and therefore repressive.[1]

She felt that her own consultancy with a staff which increasingly acknowledged differences of responsibility, in a school where the consultative structure embodied the real functional relationships, induced her to believe that teachers grow in stature in such a system, discovering new skills in themselves.

The search for consultative systems which do not coincide with the formal, permanent structure has led to experiments with variations upon both the 'formal' and the 'permanent' dimensions. These may be summarized as:

Informal/temporary	*Ad hoc* committees, working parties and study groups
Informal/permanent	'Ongoing', permanent study groups for which staff are encouraged to volunteer
Formal/temporary	Emergency use of the formal structure
Formal/permanent	Staff Councils or top management/ senior staff/full-staff group

[1] Richardson, E., 'Knowing who is boss', Article in *The Times Educational Supplement*, 19.10.73.

Some of the characteristics of these three types are examined in turn.

Informal/temporary systems

When groups smaller than the full staff group are set up to research questions, collect data and opinions and make recommendations to the whole staff group or to the head, they have the advantage that they can establish relationships more quickly, distribute tasks and engage in discussion in greater depth than a large body is capable of doing. The difference between committees, working parties and study groups is not always clear. In the practice of some schools the terms seem virtually interchangeable. There is perhaps a certain logic in regarding the term 'committee' as a possible alternative to either 'party' or 'group' except that the members of a committee have probably been elected. A working party is likely to be a committee to which has been referred a specific brief concerning a particular problem, and the task is to recommend a solution or a choice of different solutions. A study group may be regarded as having a less pre-determined role, with the emphasis upon enabling the members to develop a deeper understanding of certain issues for the purpose of placing their knowlege at the disposal of their colleagues.

It is probable that study groups or working parties are normally set up on an *ad hoc* basis and for a limited period of time. There are no universal criteria for membership. Sometimes the origin of the group lies in the eagerness for change of a self-identified group. Their wish to make innovatory proposals designates them as self-appointed volunteers and their existence becomes institutionalized as a working party. Sometimes a problem is encountered by individual teachers who may be very junior or who may be members of the top management. As a result a group has to be selected to study the matter and make suggestions. In such circumstances an effort is often made to ensure that all the appropriate interests, curricular or pastoral, are represented on the membership of the working party. On other occasions when the question is of close and equal concern to the whole staff and sectional interests are not involved, the membership may be decided by election of certain staff whose prior agreement has been obtained.

There are possible disadvantages to all these methods.

Volunteers may often come to be regarded as an 'in-gr⌐
who are seeking to promote their own interests or thei.
own ideology. Their efforts, however rational and well-
intentioned, may well lack support and authority. When
members are selected to represent others, assumptions about
the nature and extent of their representative capacity are
often remote from the reality. When any pre-existing group,
such as a department or a group of departments or a pastoral
unit, chooses a representative (or the choice is made by the
top management) to serve on a working party, that individual
requires, if he or she is to be effective, to be in a position to
speak authoritatively for the group he or she is considered
to represent. In effect this means that the representative
must either already possess or must be granted *ad hoc* leadership attributes by those represented. If the head of the pre-
existing department or pastoral unit chooses not to serve
on the working party, he or she must surrender the leadership
for the purposes of the working party to the person who
represents the leadership interests and those of the other
members of the department. In fact this rarely happens.
Representatives are often chosen because they are willing
horses, are thought to have an easier work-load than others,
or are the least likely to refuse.

When the third method of choice of membership is used
— election by the whole staff — it might be thought that this
procedure granted the members of the working party authority to work on behalf of the whole staff. Even this is no
guarantee, however, as elections can rarely be conducted in
such a way that the electors can make a firm prediction of
how the candidates will behave when they have been elected.
Moreover nominations of candidates are often made in the
hope of reducing the risk of being chosen oneself, and the
eventual choice may often be the outcome of minority votes
for the 'successful' candidates.

A more serious objection to temporary systems is they are
vulnerable to the charge that the policies which arise lack
continuity and coherence. Although a staff group as a whole
may be less subject to changing membership than it used to
be, as a result of reduced opportunities for promotion and
mobility, the changing composition of the membership of
working parties can lead to inconsistencies. After a while
the recommendations take on an air of anonymity, and
continuing responsibility for making them seems to evaporate.

Comprehensive schools, with their variety of choice in the curriculum, their broad range of pupil aspirations and performance, their large teaching staffs and frequently widely separated buildings, are in greater danger of fragmentation than the compact grammar or secondary-modern schools which they have replaced. For this reason continuity and coherence in general school policies are doubly important. No consultative arrangements which fail to take this into account can be considered entirely satisfactory.

Informal/permanent systems

There have been experiments involving the establishment of a number of permanent study groups or working parties, each identified with a basic aspect of the management such as curriculum, resources, community relations, assessment, evaluation. In such a system every staff member would be a member of one group and would state his or her preference.

Such a system is described by J. A. Johnson as being operated at the Castle School, Thornbury, Avon:

> The next mechanism to be invoked in the Castle School model of change was therefore to be the establishment of ongoing study groups to lead on from the conference and hopefully to sustain its momentum. General areas of study were designated to cover all aspects of school life, conveners were appointed for one year, and five working parties were set up for which it was hoped that the staff would volunteer. The working parties were as follows:
>
> (i) Middle School Curriculum
> (ii) Lower School Curriculum (Teachers' Role)
> (iii) Organisation and Communications
> (iv) Social and Pastoral Care
> (v) Links with Primary Schools and Community.[1]

Although at the inception of this system at the Castle School the chairmanship of each group was entrusted to members of the top management team, it was later decided to open the leadership of the groups to election. This development (as well as the principle of staff members 'volunteering' for the group of their choice) presumably marked an intentional break with the formal structure of responsibility. An additional distancing of the consultative system from the formal structure takes place and greater impermanence is

[1] Johnson, J. A., *Staff Development and In-Service Training in the Comprehensive School*, School Studies, Eastend Farm, Grovesend Road, Thornbury, Bristol, 1978, p. 39.

introduced when the task area and also the membership of each group is rotated at regular intervals with the intention of affording opportunities for gaining experience across the whole field of school tasks and also of broadening chances to establish new relationships.

Having explored informal systems, both temporary and permanent, we now come to a consideration of formal systems as the basis of consultation. Formal systems may also be analysed in categories of temporary and permanent, though 'formal/temporary' may seem an unlikely combination.

Formal/temporary systems

Such a term could only be used to describe the occasional use for consultative purposes of a body pre-existing in the formal structure but not normally consulted, and perhaps consequently possessing little realization of its collective existence. In a school which is unused to consultation of any kind, or one in which the 'middle management' (heads of department, house or year) remains unrecognized as a consultative body, the convening of such a group for an emergency, 'one-off' discussion about the distribution of resources might be described as a formal/temporary system. *Semi*-formal/temporary systems, of course, are much more common and are to be seen whenever (as described under informal/temporary systems) a working party or study group is constituted so that its members are intentionally 'representative' of units of the formal structure.

Formal/permanent systems

Before describing in some detail the machinery which might be used to activate the formal structure as a permanent consultative body, there is a sub-category to consider which might be called '*semi*-formal permanent'. Staff councils might be described in this way. Unlike working parties and study groups, which mostly have a relatively short life, staff councils often have written constitutions which make them a permanent feature of the consultative machinery. A staff council is likely to be more closely related to the permanent, formal structure of responsibility in that membership is defined in terms of representation of the sub-systems in the formal structure. Thus one or two house staff may be nominated or elected to represent the house system; a limited number of heads of departments may represent the curricular system. A staff council which reserves a proportion of places for a fixed number of teachers in the middle range of experience but without responsibilities in the formal structure is obviously deliberately departing from that structure. This is even more apparent when places are reserved for representatives of the probationer element in the staff group.

The terms of reference of a staff council are likely to be much wider than those of a working party or study group in that a staff council normally covers the whole field of school policies. Whereas a working party or study group rarely claims to represent the entire staff or to make decisions on behalf of the whole staff, a staff council may be regarded in fantasy, if not in relation to its reality, as representative of all facets of staff interests, experience and responsibilities. Consequently a staff council may be more readily entrusted with the right to vote on questions which affect the whole staff and to make decisions which are regarded as binding. Sometimes the head retains a right of veto over such decisions. If the head does not do so, there may instead be an unvoiced understanding that he or she is prepared to resign if a decision is unacceptable. In practice this must constitute quite a powerful sanction.

While a staff council which offers membership to teachers with no formal responsibility in the staff structure may be an excellent training ground and a humane device for inducting and involving new staff, offering as it does opportunities to teachers who have not yet achieved middle management responsibility, its decisions may well result in robbing the school of the leadership of all the senior and middle management staff members who are *not* members of the council. The dangers of 'by-passing' heads of department and house or year heads was mentioned in Chapter 2. All the informal systems and the semi-formality of staff councils may result in many experienced teachers in posts of responsibility being limited to the running of their own sub-systems and their being excluded from a voice in any innovatory move.

A fully permanent system of consultation, fully integrated with the formal structure of responsibility, involves the establishment of consultative groups identified with functional groups. These groups are:

(i)   the top management group (head, deputies and senior teachers entrusted with broad areas of responsibility representing facets of the task of the school);

(ii) the senior staff group (the top management group with the addition of all members of the middle management, heads of faculties/departments, houses or years);

(iii) the full staff group.

Reference to the 'full staff group' raises once more the problem of the large 'unmanageable' meeting. It was the loss of identity in such a setting and the limited chances which members are likely to have of contributing which first gave rise to the search for alternatives such as study groups and working parties. Can we not have small groups without incurring the dangers and problems of informal systems?

Small groups as part of the formal/permanent system of consultation

If what is required is small groups which represent complete cross-sections of curricular and pastoral responsibility, of age, experience and sex present in the staff as a whole, from which none is excluded and none is perceived as seeking influence which is denied to others, then it would seem logical to constitute such groups on precisely that basis. Their identification with the formal system is ensured by their permanence, by each working under the leadership of one of the top management team and by their deliberations taking place simultaneously on the same aspect of general school policy. Five or six such groups of twelve members each cater for a whole staff of 60 to 72. Six groups of fifteen each provide for a staff of 90. In groups of this size, face-to-face discussion is possible and relationships can be established which can afford the confidence which helps the youngest member to make a contribution.

If this system for organizing consultation with the entire staff is adopted, there remain a few further problems to consider. These are:

1. Is there not still a need for the whole staff to meet together as part of the consultative machinery and not solely for social purposes?

2. Under what form of leadership do the small groups operate?
3. Should small-group leadership and membership rotate or remain constant?
4. By what means can the views expressed in the small groups be brought together, compared or contrasted — and how is the head of the school enabled to become aware of the views expressed?

A number of experiments have taken place in schools in an attempt to meet these questions. Small groups of twelve or fifteen members can in practice cover most aspects of an issue in reasonable depth in a period of 45 minutes provided the time is fully used. (This is the common length of a teaching period when equally ambitious objectives are often set.) The small-group sesssion may then be followed by a plenary session of the whole staff to continue for a further 45 minutes' discussion of the same topic.

Five or six groups may suitably be led by senior staff members (the top management team consisting of deputies and senior teachers who are not identified too closely with a single subject on the curriculum or with a particular pastoral grouping).

There is a natural temptation to favour a rotation of membership and leadership of the small groups since this provides variety of contact and viewpoints and protects against the threat of having unguarded remarks 'thrown back' at one in subsequent meetings. Nevertheless the idea of the small group, stemming as it does from the need to be a known member, face to face with other known members, demands a degree of continuity both in membership and leadership. The process of acquiring skills and testing them both as leader and as member is potentially threatening and even painful. So constant changes in the constituent members of a group may provide remission of the threat at the expense of the loss of opportunities to acquire and test skills.

The head, feeling excluded from the small groups, may succumb to anxiety about how discussion is progressing and decide either to lead one group himself or herself or to visit all the groups in turn during the 45 minutes of their meeting. There are three main objections to either practice:

1. Neither visits nor the leadership of a single group can provide an adequate general picture of staff views.

2. Both visits and the leadership of a single group subtly distort by his/her very presence the nature of the discussion and the impression received.

3. Visits particularly may be perceived as distrust of free discussion by staff members and an absence of confidence in the leadership skills of other members of the top management team. (The use of the term 'leadership skills' is intended to refer to the leader's capacity to enable members to review all aspects of a problem, to become aware of its widest context and to develop ideas for meeting it, not the leader's capacity to persuade members to adopt a preconceived perspective or a predetermined solution).

The head must instead rely upon the plenary session to hear the problem explored. While the small groups are in session he or she must contain anxiety. He/she can also go over the ground in depth with the group leaders, his/her senior colleagues, at a further meeting of the executive team at the earliest subsequent opportunity. Indeed it is in this 'inner cabinet' meeting or as a result of it that a final decision can be reached. This decision will need to take full account of all the discussion of the full staff meeting and will also need to be explained and justified to all concerned. More will be said about decisions in the next chapter.

Before leaving the subject of the plenary session which should follow the group meetings, there is a further question to be examined. How does the assembled staff group of 70 — 100 members pursue its understanding of the issues under consideration and move towards the formulation of possible courses of action in such a large group — broadening without losing the insights gained in the small groups?

A procedure often favoured when small groups come together at a conference is for a spokesman of each group to 'report back' to the main meeting. This may be appropriate when a separate subject has been delegated to each group. Conference attenders will nevertheless be aware of how disappointing such 'reports' are often felt to be. A relatively brief report rarely conveys the true nature of a small-group discussion, and a long one bores the audience, which is unable to challenge, support or reject what is being said.

In addition to the inadequacy of most oral methods of 'reporting back', the procedure inevitably becomes repetitive when the small groups have all been discussing the same issue. The five or six spokesmen (usually the senior staff members leading the groups) are placed in the invidious position of either appearing to do less than justice to the hard work of the group represented or of repeating what has already been said. More serious still, the procedure obliges them to monopolize time which could have been available for the general staff membership. The latter is placed in a passive rather than a participatory relationship with the 'top management'.

When reporting back was abandoned after a trial period in the writer's school, there was not unnaturally an initial feeling that the work done in the small groups would need to be repeated in the large group in identical form if the opinions voiced in the group of twelve were to be shared with the whole staff. Indeed one teacher complained that she would be obliged to state her case twice. She withdrew this complaint when other members of her small group challenged her with the question whether their responses to her opinions expressed in the small group had really had no modifying effect upon her original viewpoint. She agreed that her opinions would now be expressed in a somewhat different form.

What has been described is a possible way of using the staff structure of responsibility as a permanent, formal consultative system. It remains to consider the kind of procedures and conditions in which consultation may be effected through meetings of top management, senior staff and the full staff group (both in small groups and in plenary session). The same procedures and conditions may be taken as applicable to departmental, house or year staff meetings, with the proviso that the smaller the group the more simplified the procedures may become. These procedures and conditions concern:

1. programming: frequency of meetings and membership;
2. agenda;
3. clarification of stages on the way to a decision;
4. distribution of preparatory information;
5. the time boundary;
6. seating as a reflection of relationships and purposes.

1. Programming: frequency of meetings and membership

The top management group (deputies and senior teachers) hold responsibilities which together with those of the head, who leads the group, cover the whole range of the aims and goals of the school. They should meet together regularly and frequently in order to ensure that there is coherence in all the school's activities. At least twice a week would seem desirable. A working lunch twice a week on fixed days may be a convenient arrangement in some schools. In others it may be considered preferable for top management to be available at such times to staff and pupils. Consequently after-school hours may be preferred for meetings. While it may be unnecessary to compile a formal agenda, opportunities should be presented to each member to report on or seek opinions about his or her own field of responsibility. A record should be kept of the topics raised. An important feature of top management meetings is likely to be discussion about the means by which information should be conveyed to and opinions sought from the members of the senior staff and the whole staff group. It may also be appropriate that bodies other than these (for instance the pupils of the School Council or the parents of the PTA or the members of the governing body) should be consulted also. The top management committee also constitutes one channel, though not the only one, through which problems, anxieties, proposals and intentions of other staff can be brought to the attention of the head. Among these may be topics of interest to the whole staff, and such subjects will then be recorded as desirable agenda for a full staff meeting. It is probably a good idea for a top management committee to reserve certain dates in their programme of meetings for consideration of long-term questions so that all procedures and policies come up for reappraisal at regular intervals.

Meetings of the senior staff and of the whole staff may both be scheduled on a monthly basis. To avoid too close proximity between meetings (since senior staff are members of both) one might be held near the beginning of each month in term-time and the other towards the middle of the month. Days on which meetings are scheduled should be varied so that the incidence falls equally on all the days of the week except probably Fridays. There are few teachers who do not have an evening course to attend or an adult evening class to take, a games practice to organize or some other duty to perform on a fixed evening in the week.

It is helpful to the forward planning of staff members if as much notice as possible can be given. A procedure which has been found useful is for a calendar of all the term dates for more than a full year ahead, four terms in all, to be placed on a notice board in the staff room. On these four sheets (one for each term) all the dates proposed for the different kinds of consultative meetings may be entered (including 'Parents' Evenings' and all other school functions). The dates appearing on the calendar of the current term and the subsequent one would normally be regarded as fixed, whereas those of the two ensuing terms would be open to discussion and amendment.

The membership of the senior staff group should be identified by the head and made clear to all concerned. It can be embarrassing for a newly appointed head of department to claim to be a member of a senior staff group if others do not so regard him. It can be equally embarrassing to miss, as a consequence of misplaced modesty, a meeting which he was expected to attend. The general purpose of identifying a senior staff group is to provide opportunities for involvement in management at as deep a level of discussion as possible for those who hold the considerable responsibility at the 'first order of differentiation' of leadership in organizing the work of other teachers. In Chapter 6, the desirability was emphasized of not differentiating between curricular and pastoral responsibilities in defining the senior staff group. Other factors which will also need to be borne in mind are the total size of the group (it should be a 'medium' rather than a 'large' group — not more than twenty-five including the top management committee) and with as reasonable a balance as possible between curricular and pastoral. A note on 'faculty' systems of organization was included in Chapter 6.

For the full staff meeting, as for the senior staff meeting, it is important to identify who are members. Is a meeting only for the *teachers* of the school? If so, are part-timers and peripatetic instrumental music teachers also invited to participate? Are members of the ancillary staff (the chief technician, the bursar, the school staff nurse and perhaps others) also welcome? It is tempting to pride oneself on a 'democratic', open-door policy and invite everybody, but the implications of doing so must be faced. Membership of a consultative management group implies responsibility as

Fig. 3 Staff notice board

AUTUMN	SPRING	SUMMER	AUTUMN
Sep 9	xxx xx xxx	xxx xx	xxx xx
10 xxx	xx xxxx	xx	xx
11 xxx	xx	xx xxx	xx
12	xx	xx	xx xxx
xx	xx	xx	xx
xx	xx	xx	xx
xx	xx xxx	xxx xx xxx	xxx xx
xxx xx	xxx xx	xx	xx xxx
xx xxx	xx	xx	xx
xx xxx	xx xxx	xx	xx
xx	xx xxxx	xx	xxx xx
xx	xx xxx	xx	xx
xxx xx	xxx xx	xxx xx	xx
xx xxx	xx xxx	xx	xx
xx	xx	xx	xx
xx	xx	xx xxx	xxx xx xxx
xx	xx	xx xxx	xxx xx
xx xxx	xx	xx	xx
xxx xx	xxx xx xxx	xx	xx
xx	xx	xxx xx	xx
xx xxx	xx	xx xxx	xxx xx
xx xxx	xx	xx	xx
xx	xx	xx	xx xxx

Current term. Dates fixed	Next term. Dates fixed	Two terms ahead. Dates negotiable	Three terms ahead. Dates negotiable

At the end of each term the left-hand calendar is removed. The other three are moved one place to the left and a new one is added, with suggested dates for three terms ahead.

much as privilege. It is confusing and inconsiderate to suggest that anyone should assume responsible membership of a group which discusses matters outside one's interests or experience. A head with his top management colleagues should therefore try to define the general nature of the issues about which a consultative group is likely to deliberate over the long term. The membership should then be defined accordingly. If the membership is decided before the kind of business to be transacted, the former is likely to influence the latter. A group designed to discuss the general management of a school may well include all the teachers and all the heads of the various ancillary services. If all adults employed in the school are deemed to be members, the business of meetings must be designed in such a way that others besides teachers are able to make an informed contribution.

2. Agenda

Oddly (in the light of the origin of the word 'agenda'), consultative meetings are not intended to be places in which things get 'done'. They should not even be places in which items of business get 'done'. They are rather places in which members examine their beliefs and ideas and those of other members and develop new dimensions of common understanding which help to weld the total body into a team with a shared commitment to the same premises. What has been described (even when a fairly practical issue is concerned) is a long process. 'Raised hands, a snap decision and move on to item 2' hardly meets the case. Since it is almost certainly self-defeating to prolong a meeting too late into the evening (the 'time boundary' is discussed later), one topic for discussion is probably all that can be managed. (Even the plural of 'agenda' is therefore inappropriate and the matter of a consultative meeting might be more suitably referred to as a 'disputandum'!).

It is not unheard of in schools for agenda to contain anything up to fifteen items. When the top management retains the authoritarian or 'tells' style of leadership, fifteen items can be disposed of quickly enough by a rapid statement of decisions already taken and a brief explanation — sometimes — of the reasons for the decisions. A move from the 'tells' to the 'consults' management style (from power-coercive to normative-re-educative) necessitates drastic pruning of the agenda. A list of items of business gives way to one topic of general concern. An attempt to discuss more than one general subject at a consultative meeting entails a number of frustrating consequences:

    (a) The management is pressured by the members (and presses itself) to curtail discussion in order to cover all the items of business promised. Members deter each other by subtle signals from expressing opinions which might prolong discussion.

    (b) Members are paradoxically much more strait-jacketed by 'items of business' than by a 'general topic of concern', as wandering off the point is a greater danger and also much more unpopular.

    (c) Management is forced back into an authoritarian mode of leadership, whatever may have been the expressed intentions.

    (d) Members become bored, restless and frustrated when placed on the receiving end of information (which could be distributed on paper) or exhortation (which is ineffective unless internal volition is already present in those exhorted). The multi-item agenda may be responsible for creating 'non-participatory' staff members. It is consistent with Maslow's theory of human need for self-realization that most people regard a meeting as valuable in direct proportion to the contribution which they have individually been enabled to make to it, whereas information and exhortation treat members as passive recipients.

The packed agenda arises from a number of practical causes. Staff meetings have in the past provided opportunities for fulfilling a number of urgent needs, covering a wide range of different topics. Other ways must be found of meeting these needs if multi-item agendas are to be replaced by a single issue of concern.

Contemporary comprehensive schools are complex institutions in which there is widespread differentiation of functions among the staff. The problems which preoccupy members are increasingly diverse. In spite of this diversity, all the concerns are interrelated. A snap decision in one area usually has far-reaching consequences affecting many other areas. Multi-item agendas are often the result of including on the business of a meeting all the individual problems which have been raised by different members. The more 'open' and 'participatory' the management, the greater is the need to demonstrate that everyone has the right to have his or her problem debated in the forum of the staff meeting. There appears to be a contradiction between a consultative and participatory mode of leadership and the selection (apparently arbitrary) of a single subject for discussion.

Problems or items of concern are likely to arise in many different ways and become known to members of the top management team by both formal and informal means. They may be expressed in a personal interview in the head's office, in a chance encounter in the corridor or on the games field, in an engineered conversation at break in the staff room, over school dinner, or in the local pub. They may be the subject of a scribbled note to the deputy head or a formal memorandum addressed to the top management team. They may have been aired at a meeting of faculty or year staff with a request that the head of faculty or year should raise the matter at a senior staff meeting or directly with the head and the deputies. With all these existing channels of communication, more formalized methods of agenda-building such as notice-board space or an 'agenda suggestions book' are probably unnecessary.

The fact remains that however they are expressed the questions which staff members wish to be considered will (or should) become known to the top management team. They will be many and varied. Some will be practical matters already clearly within established policies and satisfactorily resolved by reference to precedent. Decisions on questions of this kind where policies are not challenged can be returned directly to the originator and need not figure on the agenda of a meeting. Other problems, whether they are problems of practice or of principle, may well pose a challenge to existing policies.[1] It has been said that staff meetings are intended to promote a common understanding of shared premises; the latter kind of problem is therefore an appropriate one for discussion by the whole staff.

In the argument so far, three different terms have been used — practical problems, policies, principles. The meanings attached to these terms may be illustrated as follows by two examples drawn from different areas of management:

		Rules and Discipline	*Curriculum*
A	Practical problems	Staff on dinner duty have problems in controlling pupils' behaviour in the buildings. Grafitti, smoking and minor vandalism have increased in toilets.	Teachers of fourth-form physics sets complain of diversity of background knowledge in pupils, some of whom have done general science up until then while others have already had a year of specialized physics training.
B	Policies	To what parts of buildings should children have free access during the dinner hour?	Should there be a common curriculum in years 1-3? How open should fourth- and fifth-year options be, and what information is available to staff responsible for guidance? What teaching methods are needed in the fourth form?

[1] An analysis of the difference between 'programmed' and 'non-programmed' decisions is made in Burns, T. and Stalker, G. M., *The Management of Innovation*, Tavistock Publications, 1961.

C	Principles	At what point does independence become licence, and security and order become constrained dependency?	What is the point of balance between the motivation deriving from an absence of differentiation between younger children and the need to prepare them for public exams to which they are suited?

In determining subjects for discussion, the top management team has the task of identifying the principles which underlie the problems and the policies. It is the relationship between these general principles and management responsibilities for discipline, the curriculum, the internal organization, staff development, assessment, resources etc. which should be the subject of the staff meeting.

When problems are referred to the top management or come to their notice there should be preliminary discussions at one (or two) of their frequent routine meetings. In practice it often happens that a number of practical problems involving different policies turn out to exemplify the same questions of principle. It is remarkable that the same general principle is so often the source of major anxiety and doubt throughout a staff body even when it is unstated in its abstract form and is voiced in the form of apparently different and separate problems. In some such instances the cause can be traced to tangible origins (such as new buildings, changed examination regulations or the receipt of complaints from neighbours of the school). Often, however, it is less easy to account for the extent to which worries, in diverse contexts, embody the same fundamental and underlying uncertainty. In these cases it is tempting to conceive of a form of group consciousness which pervades the staff of a school and stirs simultaneously in individuals the same preoccupation which is translated into the separate concerns representing their varying areas of interest and responsibility.

It has been repeatedly asserted that staff meetings should never be used for exhortation or sermonizing. Internal volition and self-motivation are the products of personal conviction. Discussion of the application of principles to policies is more likely to lead to autonomous conviction than persuasion or admonition. Similarly staff meetings are not for giving information. But since the communication of information is an important responsibility of management, other ways of doing this must be found. The most common satisfactory substitute is a typewritten circular for special information and regular bulletins for routine communication.

Top management teams sometimes claim that they cannot forego the opportunity which staff meetings present to sample staff opinion on a wide variety of separate practical questions. For this reason they cannot conceive of a single-subject 'agenda'. To that objection there are two answers: first, regular discussion of principles and policies leads to much more widely shared common premises of belief and attitude which, since all staff are aware of them, render sounding of opinion on individual issues much less necessary; secondly, simpler and less time-consuming ways than staff meetings can be found for sounding out staff views on a practical proposal.

(a) The individuals concerned can be consulted for questions which are of little consequence to the majority, and executive action taken.

(b) Dates and the school calendar can be the subject of 'rolling consultation', as has already been described.

(c) The staff notice board may be used asking for initials 'for' or 'against' (on a routine issue not involving a question of principle).

(d) A circular to all staff describing a more complex proposal may end with a request for views by a given date.

(e) A subject may be discussed at a senior staff meeting and heads of faculty and year may be asked to consult their members and make a report at the following senior staff meeting.

(f) In a case of real urgency (fifth-formers have been invited at short notice to visit a rare exhibition or display in the town that afternoon and the opportunity will not recur) an announcement in the staff room may be made at break, asking for immediate reactions.

3. Stages on the way to a decision

While the position of teachers in the formulation of policy is central, the idea of the 'Educational Covenant' (Schools Council Paper No. 53, *The Whole Curriculum 13-16*) includes other parties which have an important interest in school

Fig. 4 The educational covenant

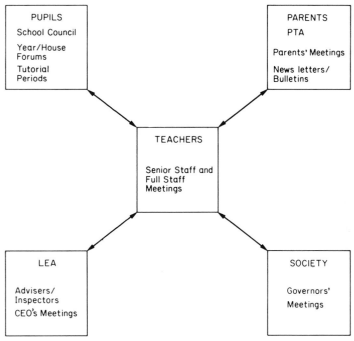

policies. These are parents, pupils, the LEA and society in general (representative opinion in a school's catchment area). On important proposals for changes of policy all of these parties may have to be consulted. Each party will need to know who else is involved in discussion and roughly when a decision may be expected. A target date for a decision is a useful device for everyone concerned as it concentrates the mind upon a purpose within a given span of time, it conveys the time limit within which influence which is brought to bear can be effective, and it enables top management to plan logically for the inclusion of all relevant bodies in the consultation during the interval left before a final decision has to be made.

The planning of consultation, whenever a number of different bodies is involved, must be systematic, and information about this intention must be clearly set out and easily intelligible. The 'flagged diagram' device is very useful for these two purposes. It shows the various meetings, whether regular programmed meetings or specially convened ones, against a time-scale as follows:

Fig. 5 Proposal to revise school uniform rules

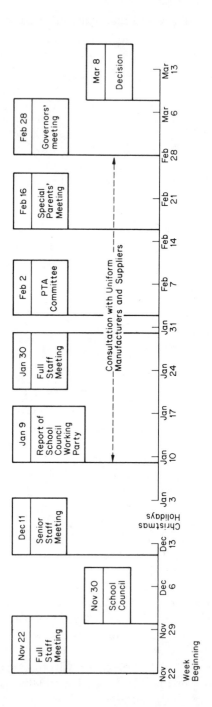

Although planning ahead for a target decision date is recommended, it must be accepted that the date cannot always be met; when (as in the case of school uniform) many different representative bodies have to be consulted, there may be a great deal of disagreement. The search for common ground may take longer than forecast. If feelings are running high one or more of the constituent bodies may demand more time and wish to hold a further meeting before reaching a view and expressing an opinion. Flagged diagrams are therefore to be regarded as a planning device proferring a tentative proposal about time limits rather than a constraining strait-jacket. The final date when a decision is hoped for may have to be postponed several times, and this should be understood and accepted by everyone concerned.

4. Preparatory information

If the purpose of a staff meeting is for members to clarify their own thoughts in the presence of their colleagues, as has been claimed, it is undesirable that the opening remarks of the head should extend to more than a brief repetition of the subject for discussion. Any longer introduction tends to set a pattern in which members constantly look to him or her for leadership and guidance throughout the ensuing meeting. The head is the titular and *de facto* chairman on such occasions and if he or she does not open the meeting at all by any kind of statement, then there is a highly embarrassing silence. This arises from the reluctance all other members feel to break the silence. They fear that the first person to open his mouth will be regarded as making a bid for the leadership and that this will be unpopular with all other members who have an equal or better right to do so. The head in this matter has a knife-edge to walk. If he or she enters and sits down without speaking, the action will probably be resented as an abdication of responsibility to get things started (or even as a malicious parlour game designed to test which member will 'break' first and relieve the tension). If, on the other hand, the head reserves the first five or ten minutes for an explanation of all the facts leading up to the meeting, members will be brought into a dependency relationship. The source of information about the problem to be examined is also far too easily looked to as the source of the solution to the problem. Indeed, once launched upon description, any leader is easily tempted across the boundary which separates description from prescription. He may find himself proposing policy changes before a single member of the meeting has had a chance to speak.

It is therefore inappropriate for the head to explain orally at the beginning of the meeting the circumstances which have led up to it. It is also inconsiderate to spring such information upon members at such a late moment and expect the expression of considered opinions. For these reasons a paper should be distributed in advance of the meeting. If people are to have time to digest it, think about it and even refer to any literature on the question which they think is relevant, the paper should be in the hands of all members at least a week before the date of the meeting.

A preparatory paper should be set out as briefly and clearly as possible. The following headings will probably be appropriate for a large number of subjects and should be set out after the date and time of the meeting and the general title of the subject of discussion:

(a) *Background information.* Here should be described the history of the school's attitude to the problem in the past (assuming that it is not a new one). The measures taken to meet it in the past may also be described. Whether it is a new problem or a recurring one, the particular instances which give cause for concern should be described.

(b) *Issues involved.* Under this heading an attempt should be made to analyse the principles (often conflicting ones) which underlie the practical problem.

(c) *Possible courses open.* In this section alternative strategies may be stated in outline form, though it is important that the paper should not enter into a detailed statement of the advantages and disadvantages of each course of action as perceived by the writer of the paper. The writer's perception is that of only one observer (or at best of the small top management team). The whole purpose of the meeting is to broaden this perception so that a wider one containing the perceptions of the whole staff management group may be formulated.

For this broadening of perception to be achieved, it is essential that all levels of management should participate and also all the different kinds of sub-systems — pastoral, curricular, academic, practical, lower school and sixth form. People's responsibilities pose different problems for them. Discussion which does not include communication of all these problems cannot successfully lead to helpful school policies. This need for all-embracing participation is one of the reasons why full staff meetings are necessary and are not adequately replaced by study groups or working parties.

The failure of a study group to broaden perceptions sufficiently is illustrated by the experience of a headmistress who set up a staff working party to make recommendations concerning school uniform. Her perception of the problem was engendered by governors' criticisms of pupils' appearance and by parents' letters of complaint to her that uniform was insufficiently enforced by teachers. Parents found it difficult to 'maintain standards' when their children told them that 'others get away with it so why shouldn't I?' In the interests of democracy, the headmistress did not attend the meetings of the working party. She was therefore surprised when the members finally produced a recommendation that school uniform should be abolished. Their perception was of the deteriorating effect upon pupil/teacher relations of the constant nagging, checking and interrogation which resulted from their attempts to enforce the rules about uniform. Apparently the teachers had been unaware of the headmistress's problems and she had been ignorant of theirs. The experience made her wonder whether to accept the working party's recommendation or reject it. The more significant question was, why there was such a gulf between her perceptions and theirs? It could and should have been bridged by frequent intercommunication between the head and the working party. Alternatively a full staff meeting would have bridged this gulf.

(d) *The time-scale leading up to a decision and other bodies to be consulted.* The preliminary paper may end with a 'flagged diagram' to convey this information whenever it seems desirable that policy changes will result from the discussion and when there is a need for a decision about the change to be made by a certain date. (Not all staff meetings necessarily aim to change policies. Often their purpose is principally or entirely the promotion of better common understanding.)

5. *The time boundary*

The starting time and ending time of meetings are matters for very careful consideration. When they have been established and until they are changed, they should be meticulously observed. A lack of formality about the starting time is not uncommon and may be an unconscious assertion that meetings are 'voluntary' (see the discussion of this phenomenon earlier in this chapter). Most staff meetings are necessarily held after the end of afternoon school. The departure of the pupils brings with it an air of relaxation. Moreover all teachers find innumerable little jobs of clearing up after one day's teaching and preparing for the next. The temptation is strong to do these jobs before going to the meeting rather than after. Both these conditions encourage unpunctuality. The more informal a head is about the starting time of a meeting, the greater the unpunctuality. A head is then encouraged to postpone opening the meeting until there are sufficient members present to justify a start, and those who have come on time are kept waiting and reflecting about all the little jobs *they* might have got done if they had not been so punctual. Next time they get their jobs done first and fewer and fewer arrive on time.

Members are dependent upon one another in ensuring a punctual start. But they are also dependent upon the head, since it is his responsibility to ensure that the proceedings start at the agreed time. That this time should itself be subject to consultation and agreement goes without saying.

Even the manner in which the start of a meeting is signalled may lead to an atmosphere that is informal to the point of casualness or may emphasize a purpose which is businesslike. If the chairman (usually the head) arrives early, intending to await the official starting time before addressing the meeting, it is almost certain that he will be drawn into individual conversation. Besides the danger that he may not notice when the starting time arrives, there is also the awkwardness of a switch from private to public, from informal to formal.

Other members too are likely to be engaged in conversation. The chairman's raised voice calling attention to the start of the meeting is likely to be intrusive and cannot fail to assume an authoritarian rather than consultative tone.

In the staff group, with the characteristics which have been implied by the argument of these pages, there will be a realization of the members' interdependence upon one another and upon the facilitating role of the top management to enable members to achieve the ends to which they are committed. The act of holding a staff meeting is itself one of the means by which these ends are identified and become common property. That the meeting should start at the time stated is also itself a desirable end which is to the advantage of all the members. The chairman who realizes this will conclude that to start on time is not authoritarian, autocratic, mechanical or inhuman. A point should be made of ensuring that the staff-room clock is accurately set (not only on the dates of staff meetings but at all times). It may be found that the best way to ensure a business-like start is to enter the staff room at exactly the starting time of the meeting, to sit down and announce the subject of the discussion in one continuous sequence of actions. A staff group which becomes accustomed to this ritual will be aware of the time and will observe the chairman's arrival. Members will have just sufficient time to conclude their own conversations while the chairman is crossing the room and silence will fall, betokening everyone's readiness to start the meeting.

A punctual ending to a meeting is equally important. For the chairman to conclude the proceedings at the agreed time is not autocratic since it is the expression of the common will. To let the discussion continue beyond the agreed time is, on the contrary, an arbitrary act deriving from the chairman's personal whim or own interest in the direction the discussion has taken. If the discussion is clearly unfinished it is better to note this and to arrange that the session be adjourned to another occasion rather than detain all the members beyond their expectations.

When a discussion is being pursued with heat and energy, it is all too easy for those who are speaking (if not for the others not participating in the particular exchange) to lose track of the time. Even if they are aware that time is running out, it is irresistible to try to get in a crushing riposte

— sometimes of several minutes' duration. It is the chairman's responsibility to bring the meeting to a close and to do so without cutting off a speaker in mid-flow. A useful device is for the chairman, who is keeping an unobtrusive eye on the clock throughout the meeting, to intervene between the comments of two speakers near the end of the time to warn that 'only two (— or three) minutes are left'. When a member stops speaking a minute or less before the ending time, the chairman may preface the remarks of the next speaker by saying 'this must be the last comment as it is nearly time'. Intervention of this kind prepares people in the way that the 'Count Down Markers' prepare drivers who are leaving a motorway.

6. Seating as a reflection of relationships and purposes

The physical orientation in which people find themselves or are placed reflects the relationship they have with one another and the purpose for which they have come together. Teachers (at least in traditionally organized classes) face all the children and all the children face the teacher. Similarly theatre audiences face the actors on the stage. Members of an audience can see little of one another, nor do they need to. In many homes today the chairs and settee are placed to face the television screen. This often results in members of a family seeing each other only obliquely. In all these settings the purpose is for communication to come from one source and to be returned from members of the group to that same source rather than to each other. The teacher, the actors and the TV screen (if it is switched on) are in dominant positions. The communication *from* them takes priority. Reciprocal communication *to* them is reduced to a minimum. Communication *between* the members of the class, audience or family is even more reduced.

A staff meeting convened so that a chairman can convey information or administer encouragement or reproof would be seated in the same way, with all the places for members facing a place reserved for the chairman. If, in addition, a table is placed between the chairman and the members, an even greater distinction is implied by the barrier, which is really more appropriate in a shop or a bank.

Teachers are so accustomed to the formal classroom setting (although mixed-ability classes and group work have brought changes) that many expect staff meetings to be conducted in a similar setting. (Indeed there may be large numbers of teachers and heads who still prefer the power-coercive relationship referred to by Chin and Benne and quoted at the beginning of this chapter.) A head who wishes to conduct a consultative (normative-re-educative) type of meeting will need to take the initiative himself or herself in planning the seating arrangements, since if this inter-vention is neglected, it is likely that the chairs will be placed in the traditional, formal pattern.

Fig. 6 A consultative setting for a meeting

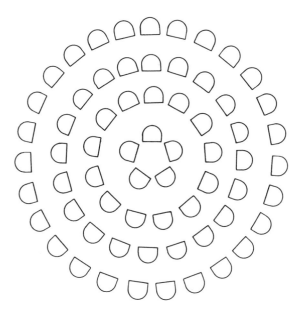

The pattern of seating which should be aimed at is one in which each individual present is able to face as many of his colleagues as possible. In a small or even a medium-sized group (given a fairly large room) this is most simply achieved by placing the chairs in a circle. Staff groups in schools of a thousand or more pupils will number anything from 70 to

120. Consequently some ingenuity will be required to attain
the face-to-face ideal or something approaching it. The
nearest approach is a series of concentric circles facing
inwards, as many as the size of the room allows. If there
are four circles, each member, by means of a normal turn of
the head, is able to address every other member with the
exception of the three who are directly in front of him or
behind. It is of no importance where the chairman is seated
as he or she has no greater expectation of addressing the
whole meeting than any other member. If the chairman
adopts the suggestion of not entering the meeting before it is
due to begin (and certainly not after that time) most, if not
all, other members will already have taken their seats. The
chairman then takes the vacant seat wherever it may happen
to be. The assumption that there will be only one vacant
seat (if all other members have arrived) arises from the care
which has been taken to set out in advance exactly the
required number of chairs. It is worth paying attention to
this apparently unimportant detail, since a shortage of
chairs leads to forays by the later arrivals into adjacent
classrooms in search of chairs, with a possible delayed start
to the discussion. The presence of too many chairs (and the
consequent empty spaces) distracts from the discussion
the attention of some members, who may speculate about
the reasons for apparent absence thus thrust into view,
and draw conclusions about the lack of urgency with which
some of their colleagues appear to regard the discussion.

In this chapter 'participation' and 'consultation' have
been understood as a mode of management and as a set of
procedures by which teachers may collectively have a share
in the making of decisions about the institution in which
they serve. An attempt has been made to justify the expenditure of time and effort which this entails on the grounds
that participation:

(a) is more effective in enabling desirable change to take
place;
(b) enhances the professional status of teachers, emphasizing their essential role as educational managers;
(c) provides conditions in which teachers' relationships
with pupils are more likely to become co-operative
rather than solely coercive;
(d) fulfils to a greater extent teachers' personal needs for
growth and development by means of a school-based

in-service training which contributes to fitting them for additional responsibility.

In the latter part of this chapter, practical questions concerning participation and consultation have been examined so that the aim of enabling teachers to share in the making of decisions may be promoted. However, in all this no mention has yet been made of the process by which the decisions are reached or the nature of the decisions themselves. This will be the subject of the next chapter.

8 Decision-Making

It has been said that the main task of leadership is the removal of uncertainty, that almost 'any old decision' is better than none. The business of leaders (pupils in controlling their own learning, teachers in their classrooms, heads of department and pastoral heads in their responsibilities, senior staff in the specific roles allocated to them and heads in general school policies) is then to make decisions — not 'any old decision' nor the 'right' one, but the one most appropriate to the circumstances of an organization and to its members. It may be important to reiterate at this point that not all consultations or all staff meetings need to be intended to lead to policy decisions. Many may have the legitimate purpose of clarifying general principles and of promoting a widely shared commitment to them. While it would be destructive to dismiss as useless any meeting which did not contribute to decision-making, it would be equally misleading to suggest that no meeting ever had this purpose. Indeed decisions are needed, and except for routine implementational matters, they should never be made without such consultation.

In the last chapter there was mention of the device of voting for or against proposals in the large staff meeting. This idea has its attractions, not least because it disperses responsibility for decisions in such a way that it is difficult to allocate blame if the results are unattractive. A severe disadvantage of the method is that proposals formulated as resolutions to be voted on must either be concocted in advance of the discussion or hastily drawn up or amended in the course of the meeting itself. The dynamics of group discussion tend to polarize viewpoints when a vote is imminent. An issue calling for sensitive analysis may receive rough and ready treatment in which a group feels itself precipitated to the necessity of choosing between two diametrically opposed courses of action. The phenomenon described in the last chapter by which some teachers become 'participators' and others 'non-participators' may all too easily reduce a group of people into traditionalists and progressives, martinets and indulgers. When it is known that a decision is to arise from a majority vote following the discussion, there is a strong temptation for members to overstate their case in order to win over the waverers. It is of course true that decisions made by an individual or by a top management team may equally well seek to implement an extreme view and may well be unacceptable to some members, or at least may not be the decision which certain members as individuals would have made themselves. But the individual or executive team can and should be accountable for their decisions in a way in which an unidentified staff majority cannot be held accountable.

The accountability referred to concerns the appropriateness of the decision to the principles which form the foundation of the aims and objectives of the school. The basic premises must not be allowed to remain matters of constant dispute, since accountability can only operate in relation to them. It is for this reason that as many meetings if not more need to be held to elucidate the principles as are held to formulate policies and promote decisions to implement them.

Some examples were given in the last chapter (under the subheadings of 'Agenda' and 'Preparatory information') of the difference between practical problems, policies and principles. The need for a decision arises from the first category of practical problems; the decision itself is a determination of policy (the second category) and this policy must be seen to be as consistent as possible with the principles (the third category).

After a meeting, the leadership (individual in the case of a department, individual and senior team in the case of a school) will require to review the views expressed in the meeting. These views are likely to embrace all three categories of problems, policies and principles. The leadership task is to marshal and assess:

1. the nature and extent of the practical problem(s);
2. possible alternative policies for meeting them;
3. the degree of compatibility of each possible policy with the principles of the school. If the latter are fully formulated they will themselves contain a strong element

of mutual contradiction and inherent incompatibility
and also be widely shared not only within a given school
but also in the educational system as a whole. For instance, a school staff may agree that their aims include:

both teacher control	and pupil autonomy
both general education	and depth through specialization
both rewards	and punishment
both curricular choice	and a common curriculum
both competitive incentives	and co-operative practices
both the promotion of excellence	and the encouragement of the average
both individuality	and a unifying *esprit de corps*
both self-confidence	and modesty
both high examination results	and self-respect for the less academic
both ambition	and a realization of one's limitations
both openness	and confidentiality
both experiment and initiative	and conformity and group loyalty

The task of marshalling and assessing problems, policy and
principles begins in a full staff meeting and is refined (in the
case of a school with an executive team) in a small top
management meeting. Even in such a small inner cabinet
meeting there may well be divergent views about the policies
preferred. If there is unanimity, it is highly unlikely that the
head will not share the unanimous view. If he/she does not,
it is obviously important to examine in what respect their
perspectives differ on the problems themselves, or on the
likely consequences of alternative policies, or on the links
between policies and principles. This examination has to continue, however protracted the process may be, until there is
general agreement.

When such agreement has been reached (sooner or later), a
wise decision will reflect the conflicting nature of the valid
principles which may motivate the management of a school.
It is therefore likely to represent a compromise. A compromise of principles is rightly regarded with distrust or even
contempt; but a compromise in policy is rarely other than
wise and desirable.

An example may be given to illustrate how policy com-
promises in decision-making can (and most frequently must)
reflect valid but incompatible principles. A former colleague
of the writer was appointed to the headship of a comprehensive school in the south of England. During a preliminary
visit, he walked around all the buildings on a tour of in-
spection with the caretaker. In a corner of the playground

they came to a wall which had a green-stained patch which extended from about three feet high to the ground. In reply to an enquiry, the caretaker explained that this marked the spot where the boys urinated during the break and lunch hour. He added 'You can't really blame the boys because all the toilets are inside the school building and the boys are locked out during their free time.' The newly appointed headmaster took the first possible opportunity after the beginning of term to consult the staff about school policy with regard to locking pupils out during break and the dinner hour.

In the ensuing meeting a number of practical problems were revealed. Certainly, it was agreed, debarring boys from access to the toilets was undesirable. This problem had not been realized. It had been assumed that they would go to the toilets before the doors were locked. But there were other problems. The school had been troubled by an outbreak of vandalism in which furniture had been damaged and displays and noticeboards covered with graffiti. Books had been taken from the library without authorization. The danger that boys might get into the science laboratories and steal harmful chemicals was particularly emphasized. Teachers patrolling the buildings could not be everywhere and experience had suggested that evacuating the buildings in free time was the best solution to the practical problem of the control of such large numbers of pupils.

Discussion of these problems led to a new awareness that certain principles underlay the conduct of the school and that these contained inherent contradictions, without being any the worse for that. Teachers wished the boys to be free within broad limits for certain things (toilets, library) but strictly controlled for others (laboratories, displays, vulnerable apparatus). Health, hygiene and decency were all principles that were accepted; but so also was the principle of safeguarding the building and its contents for the use of pupils and teachers alike.

In view of these conflicting principles, simple decisions to lock the whole building, on the one hand, or to leave it wide open, on the other hand, did not meet the case. A change of policy, which was a wise compromise, was decided upon. Boys would be allowed into the lower corridor containing the toilets; and they would be admitted by class rotation on different days to the library, which would be supervised.

(The teacher concerned would receive a lighter time-table in compensation for this duty.) On wet days the hall would be similarly supervised and quiet pursuits would be permitted. The laboratories would be locked and the main classroom areas placed out of bounds. No doubt this was not an ideal solution, because the general situation did not permit of an ideal solution. It was, however, an honest attempt to face the fact that many of our aims can only be partially achieved in an imperfect world, not simply because of the physical surroundings in which we are placed but because elements in the ideals towards which we strive are in conflict with each other. We can often reach out and grasp one principle only by totally ignoring another one. Once valid principles have been acknowledged, however contradictory they may be, the art of decision-making is to try to establish policies which provide the maximum possible advantage to the one side, combined with the minimum of disadvantage to the other side.

The assumption throughout everything which has been said about leadership is that its function is to enable all the members to become conscious of their aspirations and then to make progress towards achieving them. Consultative procedures are aimed at the clarification of aspirations; policy decisions are the instruments for trying to achieve them. The leader of a class, a department, a house or year group or a school is therefore responsible for setting up and maintaining consultative machinery (the smaller the group the less formal this need be). He or she is also responsible for making, justifying and disseminating the decisions made.

Just as it was recommended that a consultative meeting ought to be preceded by a paper giving information about the issues to be discussed, possible courses of action and the time-scale governing the whole consultative process leading to a policy decision, so the final stage of the whole series of events should similarly be marked by a carefully prepared document. This should be circulated to all members of all the different groups who have participated. For some questions not only the full staff group but also a pupils' council and a parent/teacher association committee may have been involved. Individual copies may entail a consumption of paper which will strike some teachers as extravagant; they are nevertheless essential if the close link between consultation and decision-making is to be properly recognized. In any case changes of policy which are not clearly recorded and communicated are a source of confusion and uncertainty in any institution. In large comprehensive schools where coherence and cohesiveness are only achieved by constant vigilance, uncertainty about policy decisions must be avoided at all costs. A 'decision paper' may need to be fairly long if it is adequately to record the reasons for the new decision. A brief summary should be made of the policy itself and the date when it was instituted, and this should be placed as a permanent record, in its correct alphabetically indexed place, in all copies of the 'Staff Handbook of Information'.

The decision paper itself might usefully contain the following paragraphs under the subject titles:

A. A list of the bodies involved in the discussions, with the dates on which they met.
B. A brief summary (as a reminder) of the events which occasioned the reconsideration of policy.
C. A full summary of the views expressed by the different bodies (if these showed general tendencies they may be identified). An attempt may be made to indicate the relative importance attached to different views by those consulted.
E. A review of the courses of action proposed in consultative meetings and the relationship between each and the principles which members share.
F. A statement of the preferred policy, with the reasons for the choice made.
G. Details of the necessary steps to be taken to implement the decision.
H. Suggestions about the means by which the new policy may be tested, and a date when the question will be reviewed.

The role of the governing body in decisions

Under the system of management as it is commonly practised at present, a headmaster or headmistress normally keeps the governors informed of problems and of which areas of policy are being reconsidered. Thus governors are aware of the parameters within which changes may be decided upon and give approval in advance for the head to consult colleagues and, if appropriate, parents and pupils. Knowing the consultative procedures in use, and confident that the head is aware of their general outlook and shares it, governors are normally prepared to allow heads to make all the practical policy decisions concerning internal discipline, organization and curriculum, subject to the decisions and the reasons for them being reported to them. The significant element in this procedure is that a head is enabled to follow through the logic of the consultation which has been undertaken, and it is a decision which is reported to governors, not a proposal. While it is, of course, the legal right of governors to withhold their approval of a head's report and to recommend that further consideration be given, they do not normally deprive the head of his/her responsibility to make decisions. This custom recognizes that the head's central position provides the necessary opportunities for consultation with all the interests concerned.

At first sight the recommendations of the Taylor Report[1] appear to make little change. Heads would be required to submit detailed *proposals* for change and the governors would decide whether to accept, amend or reject them. They already have this right and there seems little difference between considering a proposal or considering the report of a decision, either of which may be accepted or rejected. However, it appears from the recommendations in the report that the change is more significant. In place of a report of decisions taken by the head, the 'governing body should invite the headteacher in consultation with his staff to prepare papers setting out the means by which they propose to pursue the aims adopted' (Recommendation 39). The governing body should also have the responsibility . . . 'of making such minimum rules and sanctions as are necessary . . .' (Recommendation 40). The Committee was clearly dissatisfied with the practice by which the headteacher is placed centrally in relation to the four principal interests — teachers, parents, pupils, LEA — consults them and makes a decision. Indeed this system limits the role of a governor to being a check and balance. The Taylor Committee have in effect recommended that it is the governing body which should occupy the central, decision-making position. As the part-time, 'lay', nature of governors forbids their engaging in the kind of consultation which a head can undertake, the

---

[1] DES, *A New Partnership for Our Schools*, HMSO, 1977.

Committee envisages that the governing body should absorb
into itself elements of all the interests which a head consults.
There would be 'equal numbers of LEA representatives,
school staff, parents (with, where appropriate, pupils) and
representatives of the local community' (Recommendation 5).
The Committee's proposals would not mean the end of the
kind of consultative machinery described in the last chapter.
On the contrary, the head would be 'invited to submit general
proposals for consultation with his staff on day-to-day
matters' (Recommendation 22). The recommendations of
this report suggest, nevertheless, four very important questions. Firstly, would the views of the four (or six) teachers or
the four (or six) parents on the governing body be accepted
as sufficiently representative of the views of all other staff
members and all other parents so that the present modes of
consultation came to be considered redundant? Secondly,
assuming the continuation of present modes of consultation
– as appears to be the intention – would the indirect consultative relationship, at second hand, of the new decision-
making governing body with the main bodies consulted
afford for the new governing body the authority which is
required to make their decisions effective?

Thirdly, would the present consultative machinery, particularly that of head and staff, be viewed with the same confidence in its power to influence decisions if staff opinions were
removed by one stage from the decision-making authority?
Fourthly, would the staff members of the governing body,
constituting 25 per cent of its membership, come to be seen
as carrying more weight in the final decision-making than the
head and thus replace the head as the *de facto* leaders of the
staff consultative process?

In terms of the 'Open-System Theory' described briefly in
Chapter 2, responsibility for making decisions rests with the
leader of an organization and those of all the sub-systems
within it. Decisions of leaders of sub-systems are autonomous
provided they take account of the primary task and of the
environment in which the sub-system is placed. The recommendations of the Taylor Report introduce considerable am-
biguity into the role of the head of a school. It does not
appear to envisage a head's responsibilities as those of the
leader of an organization obliged to satisfy representatives
of the environment about his stewardship of the primary
task. Instead the governing body is seen as the leadership,

collectively accountable to no one but, in their constituent factions as teachers, parents, LEA or community nominees, accountable to the main bodies which they are held to represent.

If the Taylor Report were implemented in full, much that has been said in this chapter about decision-making would still apply to heads of department and year groups or houses but would no longer be accurate for the role of the head of a school.

This discussion of the recommendation of the Taylor Report is intended to highlight the problem of management in the context of schools and to demonstrate that the consequences of well-intentioned innovations may not always be those expected. In fact the DES document, *The Composition of School Governing Bodies* (December 1978) and the subsequent legislation rejected many of the recommendations of the Taylor Report. Notably, the then Secretary of State for Education and Science, during the second reading of the Education Bill said: 'There is still no agreement about what the formal powers of governing bodies should be. Most people, in my view rightly, see the nature of the relationship between the governing body and the school as something organic which is individual to each school. Where the relationship works, it does not need any over-elaborate delegation of statutory powers, and where it does not work, no amount of formal statutory power will increase its usefulness or its influence. The Bill, therefore, does not contain any provision relating to the specific powers of governing bodies.'

Although the government of the day decided not to give statutory expression to many of the Taylor recommendations, the spirit of much that is said in it continues to exert a strong influence upon the developing practices of the educational system, not least in the growth of systems of evaluation which are discussed in the next chapter.

9 Evaluation

The 'Green Paper'[1] affirmed that the regional conferences did not reveal any evidence of a serious decline in educational standards but acknowledged that critics claimed there had been deterioration and emphasized the need to do more than maintain present standards. After discussing the role of HM Inspectorate and the DES Assessment of Performance Unit, the Green Paper stated the need for LEAs to be able to identify schools which consistently perform poorly so that appropriate remedial action can be taken. It appealed for greater uniformity in the approach to school assessment.

'Accountability' is a concept to which teachers on the whole give assent. They accept that in education, as in all other public services, the professionals are answerable for their performance. It is when the general principle of 'accountability' is translated into 'evaluation' that opinion is much more divided.

Wolf differentiates between the two terms as follows:

> Accountability and evaluation are not the same. Accountability is dependent upon evaluation, but is a broader concept. The responsibility of accountability extends beyond appraisal, it includes informing constituencies about the performance of the enterprise. Similarly it connotes responding to feedback. Schools, however, have always had difficulty in processing data about school outputs or process performance. This is their chief problem with accountability.[2]

The Taylor Report[3] avoids the use of the threatening word 'evaluation', but in a section entitled 'Keeping under review the life and activities of the school' (6.34-6.47) it recommends (No. 45) that:

[1] DES, *Education in Schools: a consultative document* Cmnd 6869, HMSO, 1977.
[2] Wolf, R. L., 'How teachers feel toward evaluation', in House E. R., (ed.) *School Evaluation, the Politics and Process*, McCutchan, 1973, p. 156.
[3] DES, *A New Partnership for Our Schools*, HMSO, 1977.

Information and advice on the life and activities of the school should be brought together in each school with the purpose of creating an effective but unobtrusive information system for the governing body. The headteacher should be made responsible for the development of the system, working with general guidance provided by the governing body about the aspects of the school's activities on which information is required and the form in which it is required.

The Report envisages that this information should be the basis of regular reports by the head teacher on particular sectors of the school and that at longer intervals the governing body should request a 'complete and coherent picture of the school so as to appraise the school's progress as a whole and consider the extent to which its development matched their intentions.' Also (Recommendation 47) the governing body should send the LEA a short report upon the completion of its periodic general appraisal.

Whether such a process is called 'appraisal' or 'evaluation', it is unlikely to be popular with teachers at first sight. The following may be some of the reasons which may be advanced:

1. Education is such a complex activity involving so many variables and such a fragile and organic process that it is usually thought impossible to measure its success and undesirable to scrutinize it too clinically lest it perish under the microscope.
2. Our culture is now so pluralist and divided that criteria for determining what is 'good' or 'poor' performance are unlikely to command universal agreement.
3. Teachers have up to now received little training in techniques of evaluation and, in any case, are already so busy that they are reluctant to assume further responsibilities.
4. Teachers, like most people, become defensive at the thought of evaluation, seeing it as usually arbitrary, unreliable and imposed.

In order to meet these objections, schools need techniques and procedures which do not disrupt their daily life and which take account of external and semi-permanent conditions outside the schools' control. They also need supportive agreement about their aims and objectives. Next staffing ratios, financial resources and in-service training courses are required which will enable teachers to undertake the additional responsiblity of designing and operating evaluation programmes. Lastly teachers must be involved as active participants in the planning and operation so that they perceive evaluation as non-judgemental and as a contribution to the satisfaction which their work can afford them. Hayman and Napier explain that: 'Concepts of evaluation and feedback are threatening because they usually imply that something is wrong.'[1]

They urge that the concept of evaluation should be internalized and free from ideas of 'good' and 'bad' or 'win' and 'lose'. They appeal for a collaborative process of planned change, 'shared communication, data-gathering and problem-solving'. Implicit in their idea of evaluation is the power, indeed the obligation, of the evaluators inside the school to make decisions in the light of their own findings. External evaluators who identify weaknesses and thrust back upon the institution the decisions designed to remedy them form no part of their recommendations.

The planning of a school scheme of evaluation requires careful collaborative work by all the teachers on its staff. The responsibility for initiating this planning rests with the headmaster or headmistress, not least because he or she occupies the role on the boundary between the school and its environment and is the most obvious, though not the sole, channel of communication between the school and the governing body, the PTA and the LEA.

Marten Shipman recommends that the evaluation should be a responsibility delegated by the head to a senior member of staff on a permanent basis. The job will be to:

(a) Organise ongoing discussion of objectives as information is collected, tabulated and considered by staff.
(b) Organise the collection of information inside the school, its tabulation, storage and retrieval.
(c) Organise the presentation of the information to other staff, to pupils, and to the public of the school, particularly governors.
(d) Organise peer evaluation where appropriate.
(e) Organise the collection of national and local information for comparative purposes to match (a) and (c) above.[2]

[1] Hayman, J.L. and Napier, R.N., *Evaluation in the Schools: A Human Process for Renewal*, Wadsworth, California, 1975, p. 7.
[2] Shipman, M., *In-School Evaluation*, Heinemann, 1979, p. 167. This book, as well as providing an eminently practical survey of the whole subject of school-based evaluation, also offers in an appendix a list of sources of national and local statistics which may be used for purposes of comparison.

He points out that such a responsibility presupposes mathematical experience but that the central part of the job is the accumulation of information from sources both inside and outside the school.

No evaluation can take place without reference to the aims and objectives of the school. Hayman and Napier (op. cit.) describe the purpose of evaluation as follows: 'Its primary emphasis should be on clarifying the discrepancies that exist between goals and practice (intent and actuality) and on providing methods for removing these discrepancies.'

The question of drawing up aims and objectives was studied in Chapter 4. Some attempt to formulate these must precede the task of evaluation. It is nevertheless unlikely that any formulation will be totally satisfactory either in the extent of its coverage or in the classification of goals adopted. The important thing is that as many interests concerned with the school as possible should have a chance to study and contribute to the list. The senior management, or an *ad hoc* staff committee, may make the first draft compilation but it should then be open to modifications and additions by the whole staff, the governing body, the PTA and the Pupils' Council. A statement of school aims should not be regarded as permanent and unchangeable but it should not be changed too frequently either. The Taylor Report[1] recommends (No. 37) that governing bodies should set the aims of the schools for which they are responsible but that LEAs 'should alert them to the difficulties experienced, first by schools whose aims are frequently questioned and changed and, second, by schools whose aims become unalterably fixed.' (6.24).

The use of the statement of aims and objectives as a means of clarifying the discrepancies between goals and practice still poses a number of problems:

1. Many of the more important desired outcomes of education are not easily broken down into explicit statements with their own operational criteria for evaluation.

There is no really satisfactory solution to this problem but probably the extent of the difficulty has been overstated. Groups of people discussing such questions together do in practice dissect a general aim into a number of component

[1] DES, *A New Partnership for Our Schools*, HMSO, 1977.

features. In evaluating how satisfactorily the practice matches the stated intent, a range of judgements and perspectives is far from valueless even though unanimity is never reached. It must also be recognized that even an evaluation about which there remains some disagreement is preferable to an absence of appraisal. When no evaluation is even attempted, there may well be either unwarranted complacency or concealed frustration arising from undetected inadequate performance. On the other hand, there may be resentment or undue modesty arising from unrecognized good performance. In emphasizing the importance of involving a range of judgements and perspectives in evaluation, Marten Shipman (op. cit., p. 168) advises: 'Peer evaluation using local teachers in neighbouring schools, and panel evaluation by other teachers, academics and lay people should be used to supplement more conventional evaluation in areas where judgement by outsiders is appropriate.'

2. The task of schools is so wide that aims and objectives themselves, if they are sufficiently comprehensive, must be extensive. Their very copiousness must present a daunting prospect to evaluators.

This problem can only be reduced by classifying the aims and objectives in such a way that a portion can be tackled at a time. Possibly a number of committees (to include parents and pupils?) might proceed simultaneously with several different areas. Such a procedure of course gives rise to a further difficulty, which is that fragmented evaluation may result in incoherent reporting. The worst consequences of this might be alleviated by developing a central group or committee with the responsibility of drawing together opinions and recommendations which, though originating from the consideration of one category of aims, nevertheless have a bearing on several other categories.

3. The evaluation of achievements or outcomes in relation to idealistic statements of intent often, perhaps always, produces evidence of nothing but shortcomings. Such a procedure therefore appears designed to depress morale and discourage honest effort. Moreover simple comparison of intent and actuality often gives no guidance about the type of change which might be expected to improve any given outcome.

Both these difficulties point to the fact that outcomes are

not the only variables involved in education. There are two other important sets of variables. The first are the general conditions and constraints, most of which are outside the school's control, which limit the effect that the school's efforts can achieve. These may concern the ability mix of pupils in the intake, the effectiveness of contributory primary schools, school buildings and resources, parental attitudes, and the occupational and housing conditions of the community. These may be called input variables or antecedent conditions. Secondly, while some objectives may directly describe desired outcomes ('terminal objectives' describing learner behaviour), others will be 'facilitating objectives' (which may 'refer to the behaviour of someone other than the target learner. They may be procedural, but not refer directly to behaviour at all.'[1]) These may be called process variables or transactions. Acceptable evaluation takes account of all three levels of variables so that decisions are related to real rather than utopian conditions, and the day-by-day, lesson-by-lesson processes are considered in their linking role between antecedent conditions and eventual outcomes.

Hayman and Napier (op. cit.) reproduce a model from Stake[2] which shows this relationship:

Fig. 7 The Stake evaluation model

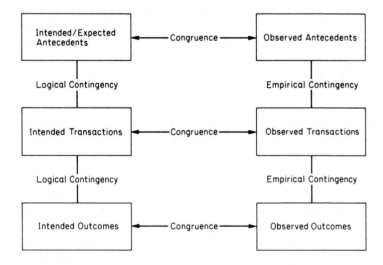

[1] Hayman, J.L. and Napier, R.N., *Evaluation in the Schools: A Human Process for Renewal*, Wadsworth, California, 1975.
[2] Stake, R.E., 'The Countenance of Educational Evaluation' (1967) *Teachers College Record*, 68, 523–40.

A whole-school evaluation must describe the general setting of the school, its physical provision, staffing, intake and surrounding community, the processes and procedures which it has adopted with the intention of achieving its goals and the resulting pupil achievements or activities. An example of this procedure as used in a research study is provided by *Fifteen Thousand Hours*.[1] 'The basic strategy of the research involved an evaluation of the ways in which outcomes are affected by school processes, after making due allowance for the effects of individual intake characteristics.' The three ingredients (inputs, processes and outcomes) are reflected in the 'items of information and advice' of which examples are given in the section (6.34 to 6.47) of the Taylor Report entitled 'Keeping under review the life and activities of the school'. The same ingredients figure much more fully in the 'Sample of a School Profile' which is set out in *Evaluation and the Teacher's Role*.[2] The checklist in this book is divided into seven interrelated sections, which are:

A. Communications System: I. Organization (Communications).
   II. Organization (Back-up and Support System).
B. Curriculum System
C. Guidance System
D. Assessment System
E. Staff Development
F. Pupil–Parent Involvement
G. Basic Considerations: I. Plant. II. The Pupil Body. III. Staffing.
   IV. Financial Provision.

Each section is sub-divided into statements ranging in number from 8 to 31. These are made in a challengeable form by the frequent use of words like 'adequate', 'sufficient', 'enough'. It is suggested that responses may be made by those participating in the evaluation in the form of: YES/NO/SOMETIMES to the more factual items and STRONGLY AGREE/AGREE/SOMETIMES/DISAGREE/STRONGLY DISAGREE to more qualitative statements.

In the Inner London Education Authority booklet *Keeping the School under Review*[3] there are thirteen sections.

[1] Rutter, M., Maughan, B., Mortimore, P., and Ouston, J., *Fifteen Thousand Hours*, Open Books, 1979, p. 43.

[2] Harlen, W. (ed.) *Evaluation and the Teacher's Role*, Schools Council Research Studies Series, Macmillan, 1978.

[3] ILEA Inspectorate, *Keeping the School under Review*, GLC Supplies Dept, 1977.

Besides covering input variables ('Simple Statistics', 'The School Environment' and 'Resources') the ILEA Guide lists process variables ('Decision-making', 'Staff Organisation', Pupil Guidance', 'Community Links', 'Arrangements for Learning'). Outcome variables are covered by eight out of sixteen items in the 'Simple Statistics' section. There are further sections for self-assessment by a department or faculty, by the head teacher and by the individual teacher. The ILEA Inspectorate offer the guide as a brief survey designed to stimulate teachers to consider their own views on what the secondary stage of education is about, taking account of the general climate of opinion in society at large. It is assumed that self-assessment will inevitably contain both fact and opinion.

Evaluation is a process which, as the ILEA guide reveals, may be conducted at the level of the whole school, at the level of a sub-system such as a department or pastoral unit, or at the level of the interactions of an individual teacher with a single class. The smaller the unit concerned the more subjective the self-appraisal tends to be and the greater the need for other people's independent views to be available. In proportion also is the increase in the sense of threat, which is more sharply personal and less widely shared. As the unit of evaluation diminishes in size so there is a need for increased attention to be paid to creating an atmosphere of openness and trust for both these reasons. A department or an individual teacher is more likely to co-operate in evaluation which involves the opinions of others if:

1. The person(s) assessed assents to or initiates the area to be evaluated and the criteria to be adopted and selects the evaluator.
2. Assessment is factual rather than judgemental, quantitative rather than emotive.
3. It is agreed that the data assembled is primarily for the use of the one(s) assessed and will not be disclosed without prior agreement.

When and if the active co-operation of those concerned can be freely given an independent evaluator may prove helpful. A department might seek the assistance of the head of some other department. The 'external' evaluator of an individual teacher is most naturally his/her own head of department. If, for personal reasons (it is to be hoped very rarely), a teacher cannot accept the head of department as evaluator, a staff tutor (if such an appointment exists), a deputy head, the head, or another department head of a related subject might prove acceptable. A staff tutor or deputy head or head would be an appropriate evaluator for heads of department and pastoral heads. Deputy heads and heads could no doubt engage in reciprocal evaluation, but wider staff and parent views are relevant too.

When classroom performance is being evaluated, pupil opinion might be sought when conditions are favourable. Pupils' opinions expressed in scaled assessments of a teacher's effectiveness are unlikely to be either accurate or acceptable. On the other hand identification by pupils of which (listed) procedures used by the teacher they find most helpful to their learning and which least helpful may furnish the teacher with valuable guidance for future lesson planning. Heads of department might welcome in-service training in the use of observational techniques. Hayman and Napier (op. cit.) mention category systems,[1] the 'who to whom' method of recording group talk and the CERLI Verbal Classification System.[2]

Regular, perhaps annual, self-appraisal interviews may be instituted as a part of the role specification of appointments at all levels. When a programme of individual evaluation of this kind is established, it must clearly form an integral element in a staff-development scheme. No form of evaluation should be separated from decision-making. Individual evaluation is merely data-gathering. The decision-making arising from it is staff-development.

The survey of the scope of evaluation which has been attempted here has emphasized that the aim should be to bring all school activities under review in a systematic way. These activities include both the long-term and long-range services provided and also the relatively short-term units of classroom teaching. If such evaluation is to be thorough and involve everyone concerned, not too much should be attempted at any one time. A full review is unlikely to be completed in a cycle of less than four years. For this reason the process has to start with consultation about the priorities of the programme itself. When these are established and the programme itself begins, a carefully devised recording system will be

[1] Simon, A. and Boyer, G., (eds), *Mirrors of Behaviour: An Anthology of Observational Instruments*, Research for Better Schools, Philadelphia, 1967.

[2] Published by the Cooperative Educational Research Laboratory, Inc.

needed to ensure that all the information gathered is constructively utilized. Harlen suggests that recording might take the following outline form:[1]

Fig. 8 Profile of school services (Harlen)

Service which may be provided	Evaluation	Details of service actually provided	Remedial action proposed
School records are adequate to show details of all individual pupils' progress	Yes/No/Sometimes or SA/A/Sometimes/ Disagree/SD	A school record does exist but this is thought to be inadequate	A staff committee will be set up to recommend changes in the system of records

Marten Shipman (op. cit. pp. 165 and 166) summarizes the characteristics of a satisfactory programme of in-school evaluation in the form of six recommendations. They may be reported as follows:

1. Evaluation should be considered as an integral part of the total organization for learning, not tacked on as an optional extra.
2. Evaluation should be accepted as being about judgement, not just the production of statistics.
3. Evaluation should employ a variety of viewpoints. There is a place for a number of different perspectives on the same aspect of school life.
4. Since teachers carry the responsibility, they should take the initiative for evaluation. It not only improves effectiveness; it is the guarantor of professional autonomy.
5. Data-gathering has to be systematic, arising from the need to obtain the maximum information from minimum effort.
6. Staff have to have a commitment to evaluate. A reluctant approach will ensure failure.

It is partly because systematic evaluation necessarily implies changes that the concept provokes resistance. It is often said that teaching is one of the most conservative of professions. This is true not solely because an important part of its responsibility is to transmit the culture, skills and knowledge

[1] Harlen, W., *Evaluation and the Teacher's Role*, Schools Council Research Studies Series, Macmillan, 1978, p. 128. Reproducted by permission of Macmillan, London and Basingstoke.

accumulated in the past but also because its organization, its forms of control and the privacy and isolation of its work in the classroom all constitute characteristics which contrast diametrically with those associated with innovation. It would, however, be quite wrong to suppose that resistance to change is the only wind blowing in the atmosphere of a school. Nor would it be true that teachers are alone in yearning for stability. Pupils, parents and local education authorities too can often adopt very hostile attitudes towards proposals for change. All the elements in the educational system display both radicalism and conservatism. It is important that this should be recognized so that no single element in the system becomes imprisoned in a polarized identification with either, on the one hand, a radicalism that embraces changes for their own sake or, on the other hand, a conservatism that refuses to contemplate any kind of change. In practice, despite the apparently inherent conservatism of school systems, teachers themselves press for more organic structures, a system of consultation and participation and the institution of 'temporary systems' such as study groups and working parties. All these have as their justification the fact that they facilitate change. Elizabeth Richardson noted the ambivalence by writing: 'For any member of staff who might say desperately to the headmaster: "Don't change anything else!" there could be another who says: "But we haven't really changed anything yet!" '[1]

No doubt comprehensive reorganization initially gave rise to a proliferation of changes, often hastily conceived, in the curricular and organizational practices of schools. The purpose of systematic evaluation is not to open the flood-gates to unnecessary changes but, on the contrary, to limit changes to those practices which general agreement concedes require reform in the interests of all the parties concerned.

---

[1] Richardson, E., *The Teacher, the School and the Task of Management* Heinemann, 1973, p. 351.

10 The Essence of Leadership

Much of what has been said in the preceding chapters has inevitably focused on areas of responsibility, tasks and decisions. Although it has been impossible to discuss these without implying attitudes, assumptions and beliefs of what leadership (or management) is for, it may be worth while devoting this concluding chapter to an attempt to identify the essence of the standpoint from which these chapters have been written.

In the first place this book has not been about headship. It may well be that the title has led some to read it with that expectation. It has instead been about *all* teachers specifically, and it has also been more generally about the leadership exercised in different spheres by pupils, parents, governors, local authority officers, elected members of education committees and others.

Leadership is associated with responsibility for a task. In education different responsibilities are widely dispersed among people with different functions. It is, of course, true that these responsibilities vary in scope and in the impact they make upon the person or persons responsible. What is occasional, less sharply defined and often largely unconscious for the parent is full-time and ever-insistent for teachers in senior management roles. According to Elizabeth Richardson:[1]

> The authority of the head cannot, therefore, be studied in isolation: it must be understood in relation to the authority of every local education officer, every school governor, every teacher, every parent and every pupil who is connected with the school.

The interdependence of all these people engaged in their different ways in the task of education is what gives rise to the strong emotions which are often evoked when their

[1] Richardson, E., *Authority and Organization in the Secondary School*, Schools Council Research Studies Series, Macmillan, 1975, p. 120.

relations with each other are discussed. All are at different times and in different ways taking leadership roles. In the last analysis, leadership is concerned with the power to make decisions, and these may have far-reaching effects working to our advantage or to our disadvantage. David K. Cohen points out that 'Decision-making, of course, is a euphemism for the allocation of resources − money, position, authority and so on.'[1] It is not surprising therefore that there is constant competition between all the individuals and all the parties concerned to acquire or to retain and to exercise the power which they possess to make decisions. In matters in which they do not estimate as high their chances of acquiring the right to decide, they nevertheless compete to influence the decisions of others. In this country, as in the USA, 'Schools are vulnerable institutions. They operate constantly at the focal point of conflicts.'[2]

Evidence of the struggle to shift the locus of decision-making is provided by the Taylor Report's recommendations, Numbers 37 and 40, particularly, concerning the curriculum, school rules and sanctions. Further evidence was the study undertaken by the National Union of Teachers in 1971.[3] Their analysis of possible machinery for participation envisaged a transfer of decision-making in certain areas from the head to either the full staff meeting, to an elected staff committee, an *ad hoc* non-elected committee, an academic board or a staff council. Their discussion of consultation was concerned with the extent of the power of teaching staff to influence decisions.

Perhaps the struggle to acquire the powers of leadership is less constructive and, in the end, the identity of the victor(s) and the vanquished is less important than an understanding of the responsibility involved. This is multi-dimensional whoever fulfils it. No one party in the educational enterprise has the right to make decisions which favour its own sectional interests to the detriment of the others. It is a truism to say that all that counts is the interests of the pupils: but the statement suffers from oversimplification. Dissatisfied parents make dissatisfied pupils; disregarded teachers make

[1] Cohen, D. K., 'Politics and Research' in House, E. R. (ed.) *School Evaluation, The Politics and Process*, McCutchan, 1973, p. 97.

[2] Hoke, G., 'An Evaluation "needs assessment"' in House, E. R. (ed.) *School Evaluation, The Politics and Process*, McCutchan, 1973, p. 32.

[3] NUT, *Teacher Participation: A Study Outline*, NUT, Hamilton House, Mabledon Place, London, 1971.

badly taught pupils; ignored governors and a school out of touch with its environment (and accordingly distrusted) make disadvantaged pupils; a powerless local education authority is reluctant to vote resources upon which the welfare of pupils depends. While there may be evidence that not all heads exercise their leadership and decision-making powers in a way that satisfies all the interests with a stake in the school, it seems improbable that a transfer of the leadership to any of the other groups involved would achieve that very desirable result. It is not the intention of this survey to introduce any bias into the discussion of *where* decision-making power should rest, but rather to suggest that a consultative mode of leadership is required whoever exercises it. In a system which allows and encourages every interest to assist in the formulation of views, it is more likely that decisions will reflect the total task in a multi-faceted perspective, rather than a 'tunnel-vision' or myopic one. This is a system which, wherever formal power may be located, attributes rights of leadership to all, shares the exercise of leadership and promotes the study of the skills required.

Such skills have a great deal to do with an understanding of ambivalent feelings and with handling incompatible ideas and attitudes. Ability to use one's leadership constructively depends in the first instance upon an avoidance of the traps set by projection and polarization. To identify radicalism with a certain section of the teaching staff and conservatism with another, to attribute appraisal and evaluation rather than support and interest to either governors or the inspectorate, to split caring and enabling on the one hand from administering and organizing on the other on the dimension of the pastoral/curricular sub-systems or that of the male and female deputy-head roles, to treat inclinations towards participation and non-participation or towards innovation and stability as pre-determined personality or group characteristics — to do any of these things is to foster the very conflicts which handicap and even immobilize constructive leadership. Every individual is prone to the need for an identity. This identity is most easily defined by contrast with an opposing one. The task of leadership is often thought to consist in codifying a set of divisive beliefs which provide a group identity, in stimulating loyalty to these beliefs and in inciting hostility to everything else. This kind of leadership is inevitably destructive and thrives in an atmosphere of insecurity.

The essence of the task of constructive leadership is to foster a climate of security and openness which enables identity and corporate commitment to flourish without the need for scapegoats and adversaries.

Elizabeth Richardson expresses this with reference to the head of a school, but what she says is equally true of all individuals and groups fulfilling a leadership role:

> For it is in the head of a school that the waves of controversy about what the future pattern of education should be collide most forcefully and painfully. The head, it seems, must be secure enough in himself to contain conflicts between the generations, conflicts between different social classes, conflicts between teachers and administrators, and conflicts between different political parties in the area, while still retaining his own personal and professional perspectives upon the educational task as he manages his school . . . Is it enough, then, to say that heads of schools have to take into themselves the tensions that rightly belong to others? . . . Is it enough to say, with a mental shrug, 'All right: this is what a head is paid to do?' Do we not rather have to help people, both inside and outside the school, to take personal responsibility for their own insecurities and indeed for their own split feelings? Leadership at any level has to acknowledge this kind of help to be part of its task.[1]

[1] Richardson, E., *Authority and Organization in the Secondary School*, Schools Council Research Studies Series, Macmillan, 1975, p. 119.

Further Reading

Barry, C. H. and Tye, F., *Running a School*, Maurice Temple Smith, 1972.

Blackburn, K., *The Tutor*, Heinemann, 1975.

Harlen, W. (ed.), *Evaluation and the Teacher's Role*, Schools Council Research Studies Series, Macmillan, 1978.

Hoyle, E., *The Role of the Teacher*, Routledge & Kegan Paul, 1969.

Hughes, M. G., *Secondary School Administration: A Management Approach*, Pergamon Press, 1974.

ILEA Inspectorate, *Keeping the School under Review*, G.L.C. Supplies Department, 1977.

Marland, M., *Departmental Management*, Heinemann, forthcoming.

Marland, M., *Head of Department*, Heinemann, 1971.

Marland, M., *Pastoral Care*, Heinemann, 1974.

Open University, *The Curriculum: Context, Design and Development*, Course E283, Open University Press, 1972.

Open University, *Curriculum Design and Development*, Course E203, Open University Press, 1976.

Poster, C., *School Decision-Making*, Heinemann, 1976.

Richardson, E., *The Teacher, the School and the Task of Management*, Heinemann, 1973.

Richardson, E., *Authority and Organization in the Secondary School*, Schools Council Research Studies Series, Macmillan, 1975.

Rutter, M., Maughan, B., Mortimore, P., Ouston, J., *Fifteen Thousand Hours*, Open Books, 1979.

Shipman, M., *In-School Evaluation*, Heinemann, 1979.

Index